D0055382

Gestapo

Gestapo

THE STORY BEHIND THE NAZIS' MACHINE OF TERROR

LUCAS SAUL

ARCTURUS

AKG: 81

Bild Archiv: 51

Getty Images: 5 (Keystone-France); 9 (ullstein bild); 10 (Bonwitt/ullstein bild); 14 (Fox Photos); 19 (ullstein bild); 28 (heritage Images); 32 (ullstein bild); 39 (PhotoQuest); 49 (Universal Images Group); 62 (Keystone); 72; 83 (ullstein bild); 88 (Keystone); 105 (Keystone/Hulton Archive); 115 (Keystone); 122 (Popperfoto); 131 (Keystone); 144 (Keystone); 150 (ullstein bild); 167 (Paul Popper/Popperfoto); 173 (Popperfoto); 175 (ullstein bild)

Hulton-Deutsch Collection/Corbis Images: 177

Reuters/Corbis Images: 93

Topfoto: 85 (ullstein bild): 99

Wikimedia Commons: 47

ARCTURUS

This edition published in 2016 by Arcturus Publishing Limited
26/27 Bickels Yard, 151–153 Bermondsey Street,
London SE1 3HA

Copyright © Arcturus Holdings Limited/Lucas Saul

All rights reserved. No part of this publication may be reproduced, stored in a retrieval system, or transmitted, in any form or by any means, electronic, mechanical, photocopying, recording or otherwise, without prior written permission in accordance with the provisions of the Copyright Act 1956 (as amended). Any person or persons who do any unauthorised act in relation to this publication may be liable to criminal prosecution and civil claims for damages.

ISBN: 978-1-78599-127-1
DA004672UK

Printed in China

CONTENTS

INTRODUCTION
BIRTH OF A MONSTER

In the films, they are the men in black leather trench coats, knocking on doors in the middle of the night and arresting anyone who dares to threaten the Third Reich. But who, exactly, were the Gestapo? How did they fit into the Nazis' oppressive regime, and why did they become so powerful, so effective and so feared?

The true picture is inevitably more complicated than the myth. The men of the Gestapo, though often accountable only to themselves and their immediate superiors, did not work in isolation. They shared a single chain of command with their sister organization, the *Sicherheitsdienst*, or SD. The SD was the intelligence agency of the *Schutzstaffel*, or SS, Hitler's protection squadron. The SS and the Gestapo are frequently confused, which is hardly surprising given that they worked in close co-operation throughout the war. The SS swore its allegiance to Hitler and the Reich, whereas the Gestapo was, ostensibly, the secret state police for Germany. To confuse matters further, there was also the *Kriminalpolizei* ('Kripo'), which handled purely criminal matters in Germany. Like the Gestapo, they were answerable to the Reich Security Main Office (*Reichssicherheitshauptamt*, or RSHA). The Gestapo and Kripo were collectively known as the *Sicherheitspolizei* (Security Police) or 'Sipo'.

To some extent the distinctions between these different organizations are artificial: the chief investigators at the Nuremberg trials concluded that applicants for positions in the Gestapo, SD and Kripo received similar training and co-operated so closely as to often be indistinguishable from one another. All were concerned with combating perceived 'enemies of the Reich' and, as the war progressed, they all operated far beyond anything that could be called the rule of law. In broad-brush terms, the SD could be considered to be an information-gathering agency and the Gestapo the executive agency of the police. The Gestapo's targets were political and ideological enemies of the Reich, while purely criminal activity was left for the Kripo to handle.

The monster that the Gestapo became was born on 26 April 1933, when the new Minister of the Interior for Prussia, Hermann Göring, was charged with creating an effective political police force. On 30 November 1933, Göring issued a decree stating that the new force would be answerable only to him, and to the Reich. All other police authorities would be subordinate to it. A further decree on 8 March 1934 separated the regional state police offices from their district governments. To complete the job of forming a nationwide extra-judicial organization, a decree on 10 February 1936 declared that orders of the Secret State Police were no longer subject to the review of the administrative courts. The new, all-powerful force was now also tasked with investigating crimes against the Nazi Party as well as against the German state.

On 1 October 1936 this new force received a new name: the *Geheime Staatspolizei*, or Gestapo for short. The name means 'Secret State Police'. In fact, the Gestapo served the Nazi Party and the leadership. Göring relinquished control of the force in order to take charge of the Luftwaffe (air force), at which point Heinrich Himmler became the overall Chief of the German Police. The first Chief of the Security Police (and SD) was Reinhard Heydrich. The different police and intelligence forces were later centralized under the Reich Security Main Office (RSHA).

Bureaucracy at the Heart of the Gestapo

One of Göring and Himmler's first tasks had been to imbue the political police force that they inherited – which was subject to judicial review and staffed by criminal investigators concerned with protecting the German state rather than any political party – with a Nazi ideology. Through Heydrich, they espoused the view that since the Nazi Party represented the German people, defending the interests of the party was the

Reinhard Heydrich

Described by Hitler as 'the man with the iron heart', Reinhard Tristan Eugen Heydrich was chief of the Reich Security Main Office, which included the Gestapo, and founder of the *Sicherheitsdienst* (or SD, the intelligence agency of the SS). Born in 1904, he was handed control of the Gestapo by Heinrich Himmler in 1934. One of Heydrich's first operations was the 'Night of the Long Knives', when some 200 members of the rival para-military *Sturmabteilung* (SA) force, including its leader Ernst Röhm, were executed.

Heydrich set about organizing the Gestapo into a national and international instrument of terror. He established a system of colour-coded index cards for keeping information and monitoring the movements of perceived enemies of the Nazi state. He also instigated the so-called 'Night and Fog' disappearances of 'persons endangering German security'. Through such actions, the words 'Gestapo' and 'terror' would become synonymous.

In 1942 Heydrich chaired the infamous Wannsee Conference, which formalized plans for the 'Final Solution' or Holocaust. Shortly afterwards, he was assassinated by a team of British-trained Czech and Slovak soldiers. He was buried with full military honours, though Hitler railed in private that Heydrich had been 'stupid and idiotic' for driving around in an unarmoured open-top car. At least 1,300 people were massacred by the Gestapo in retaliation for Heydrich's murder.

same as defending the interests of the people. The Gestapo's key legal counsel, Werner Best, described the organization as a 'doctor to the German body', keeping a watchful eye on any 'symptoms' that might lead to the nation becoming 'sick'. It was a stroke of genius, allowing the Nazis to imply that the life or death of the German people was in the hands of the Gestapo. The political police were no longer to be viewed as investigators of crimes but as protectors of the nation's well-being.

Initially, the spine of the Gestapo was recruited from the Prussian political police, and had a modest size of around 1,000 employees. Regional Gestapo offices tended to be located in dense urban areas or at key strategic border zones. There were 64 such offices at the outbreak of the war. The number increased as the Reich expanded into new territories, but there was also a drive to centralize authority, so many smaller regional offices were merged together. For this reason the total number of Gestapo offices remained in the dozens rather than the hundreds, even at the height of the Reich.

In terms of personnel, the organization grew rapidly throughout the 1930s: there were an estimated 6,500 Gestapo officers across the Reich by 1937. The outbreak of war brought a new urgency to the expansion process and the number of officers swelled to 15,000 by late

1941. The sheer size of the organization necessitated a radical restructuring, and Himmler used the opportunity to further strengthen the ties between the Gestapo and the SS by bringing them together in one building. Hence the RSHA opened in September 1939.

There were six (from 1941 it became seven) separate offices at the RSHA: Personnel (I), Administration (II), German Lands (III), Combating Opponents (IV), Fighting Crime (V), Foreign Intelligence (VI) and Ideological Research (VII). The first two departments were the bureaucratic heart of the organization, responsible for the day-to-day running of all other departments. Office V was the headquarters of the Criminal Police, while Offices III, VI and VII evolved from former SD agencies.

Office IV was dominated by Gestapo personnel. It had a reputation for dynamism and flexibility, which meant that its exact areas of influence were not easily defined. As the war progressed, Office IV absorbed former SD offices and extended its reach into almost any area it considered important to the survival of the Reich. Heinrich 'Gestapo' Müller was trusted by Himmler and Heydrich to 'get the job done', no matter what it involved. As a result, when the chaos of war enveloped Germany and its police forces, an increasing amount of responsibility was handed to the Gestapo.

Heinrich ('Gestapo') Müller

Known as 'Gestapo Müller' to distinguish him from another SS general of the same name, Heinrich Müller was born in 1900 to working-class Catholic parents in Munich, Bavaria. He was awarded the Iron Cross for his service as a pilot during the First World War, and went on to become the head of the Munich Political Police Department during the Weimar Republic. He was initially hostile to the Nazi Party, describing Hitler as 'an immigrant unemployed house-painter', but his diligent work nonetheless brought him to the attention of Reinhard Heydrich, chief of the Reich Security Main Office. Müller was a workaholic who knew how to follow orders – an ideal puppet for the Nazi leaders. In time, his eagerness to impress his superiors led to him becoming reviled as one of the chief architects of the Gestapo's worst crimes.

Müller joined the SS in 1934, and by 1936 had risen to become the Operations Chief of the Gestapo. Throughout the Second World War he helped oversee the transportation of Jews and other 'undesirables' to the Nazi concentration camps. He was Adolf Eichmann's boss and intimately involved in the detailed planning of what became the 'Final Solution'. In addition, Müller was responsible for co-ordinating much of the espionage and counter-espionage activities of the Gestapo. He successfully infiltrated the 'Red Orchestra' network of Soviet spies, and ordered the execution of over 200 people alleged to have been involved in the plot to assassinate Hitler in July 1944.

Müller remained confident of a Nazi victory right up until the very end of the war, at which point he disappeared from Hitler's bunker and was never seen again. A later CIA report concluded that he was probably killed in Berlin shortly after the war, but there is no conclusive proof of this. He remains the most senior Nazi figure never to have been captured or confirmed as dead.

The damaged Reich Security Main Office, Prinz-Albrecht-Strasse, Berlin in 1945.

Throughout its history, the internal organization of Office IV changed frequently, as the demands placed upon it shifted. For the majority of the time, however, it consisted of six groups, usually referred to by letters of the alphabet. Group A handled Political Opposition, B Religious Dissent, C Protective Custody & Press, D Occupied Zones, E Counter-intelligence and F Foreigners. These groups were themselves further subdivided into six sections (Group IV B section 4, for example, handled Jewish matters and was headed by Adolf Eichmann).

Such a bureaucratic structure required a large team of civil servants and administrative staff. Indeed, the majority of Gestapo employees were not fanatical Nazis inspired by

Himmler's ideological training, but everyday German citizens attempting to provide for their families. Many were also driven by a genuine belief in protecting the German state from the corrupting influence of communism. In the early stages of the Gestapo's history, the chief focus was on the political enemies of the Nazi Party and so employees with experience of anti-communist activities were actively sought. Veteran criminal-police officers of the Weimar Republic were also recruited into the Gestapo in large numbers, and many welcomed the fact that they could operate with limited judicial oversight because it allowed them to get their jobs done more easily.

Intermingled with such veteran police officers were ambitious young legal administrators who bought into the Nazi ideology and made sure their superiors were aware of their loyalty to the cause. This 'new blood' that flowed into the Gestapo had no first-hand experience of war, and generally came from well-educated middle-class backgrounds. Many had studied law at university, and were entering the workplace for the first time. Remarkably, however, there was relatively little tension between the very different types of employees working for the Gestapo. This unity was one of the great strengths of the organization, and one of the key reasons for its astonishing success.

CHAPTER ONE
THE EARLY YEARS

The focus of this book from here onwards is not on the
Nazi bureaucracy that lay behind the Secret State Police,
but on the brutal actions of that force. For, in the words
of its first chief Reinhard Heydrich, the Gestapo:

*... are still adorned with the furtive and whispered secrecy
of a political detective story. In a mixture of fear and
shuddering – and yet at home with a certain feeling of
security because of their presence – brutality, inhumanity
bordering on the sadistic, and ruthlessness are attributed
abroad to the men of this profession.*

A taste of things to come

The Gestapo's main focus in the early years of its history
was the destruction of its political enemies. Communists
topped the list, but Hitler also feared that some of those
within his own party had grown too powerful, and he
wanted them eliminated. The veneer of judicial process
was maintained by the establishment of the 'People's
Court', which opened on 1 July 1934. Hitler was frus-
trated by the judicial system bequeathed to him and
wanted a 'kangaroo court' to do his bidding. Most
Gestapo prisoners found themselves in the dock of the
People's Court, where show-trials were held to convince
the German people that due process was being followed.

Even this early in its history, the Gestapo had a strong presence in the concentration camps that would later come to epitomize the horror of the Nazi regime. The Gestapo had an office at Dachau, where detailed records of prisoners were kept along with the transcripts of interrogations. Registrations, identifications, admissions and releases were all overseen by Gestapo chiefs. Their underlings were generally SS men; the Gestapo chiefs were themselves nominally subordinate to the camp commandants.

The Gestapo also advised on camp security, both in the concentration camps and in the prisoner-of-war camps that soon sprang up across the Third Reich. And they ran their own 'work education camps'. These detention centres were initially used to punish 'shirking' workers for short periods of time, but later all manner of minor crimes could result in offenders being sent to them for 're-education'.

It was inevitable that such treatment would sound a warning bell, causing discontentment and anger in many and leading to dissent.

The Reichstag Fire

In 1933, just four weeks after Adolf Hitler had been sworn in as Chancellor of Germany, the historic German parliament building the Reichstag was deliberately burnt down. This was a propaganda gift for the Nazi Party,

The Reichstag building during the devastating fire of 1933.

which had long warned of the danger of a communist insurrection. Indeed, many historians dispute the official explanation that a young Dutch communist called Marinus van der Lubbe plotted the arson attack on his own. Herman Göring was said to have publicly boasted of having planned the attack as a 'false flag' operation to whip up hysterical fear in the German population.

Certainly the effect of the fire was to grant the Nazi Party unprecedented power, as Hitler immediately forced through the so-called Reichstag Fire Decree, which suspended many of the key civil liberties in Germany. Thousands of communists were rounded up and imprisoned, and countless more were prevented from voting in the hastily arranged fresh elections, which saw the Nazis increase their majority of the vote and consolidate their new-found power. The fear of a communist plot succeeded in pushing the population to the extreme right, and by suppressing their main rivals, the Social Democratic Party, the Nazis were able to secure the two-thirds majority required to pass the Enabling Act. This gave Hitler the power to rule by decree. Democracy was at an end, and the dictator Adolf Hitler was now free to march the country to war.

Five communists were tried for the attack on the Reichstag, but only van der Lubbe was found guilty. Hitler was furious and promptly ordered the establishment of the People's Court (*Volksgerichtshof*), which would be under his direct control. His Minister of the Interior, Herman Göring, re-ordered the police force into a paramilitary group of loyal Nazis, and on 26 April 1933 a decree was issued to officially create the Secret Police Office.

It was to become the most notorious secret police force in history.

Night of the Long Knives

Although the Enabling Act had granted Hitler absolute power over the German people, he still feared that his position was vulnerable. The rise of the Nazi Party had been predicated on forming alliances with those who did not share Hitler's vision for the future of Germany, and internal dissent now represented the greatest threat to the dictator.

Two figures in particular were at the top of Hitler's hit list for elimination. Gregor Strasser led the left-wing ('Strasserist') wing of the Nazi Party, which pursued an anti-capitalist agenda of social reform. Ernst Röhm was head of the *Sturmabteilung*, also known as the SA, or 'Brownshirts'. This paramilitary force had been vital in facilitating Hitler's rise to power but it had now grown so powerful and out of control that it threatened his own military units. In addition, the short-tempered

Röhm had referred to Hitler as 'the ridiculous corporal' when ordered to acknowledge the subordination of the SA to the *Reichswehr* (or 'Reich Defence', the forerunner of the German armed forces or *Wehrmacht*). The crunch point came when German president Paul von Hindenburg threatened to impose martial law if Hitler failed to control the almost daily street battles between the Brownshirts and the communists. In late June 1934, Hitler decided to eliminate all his opponents in one fell swoop. To carry out the purge he turned to his newly formed secret police force, the Gestapo, and the SS.

The codeword 'Hummingbird' was used to send the death squads into action. The list of targets had been drawn up by Heinrich Himmler and Reinhard Heydrich, with Hermann Göring and top Gestapo official Willi Lehmann adding the names of 'undesirables' outside of the SA. Lehmann would personally take part in the murderous rampage that followed. He himself would later fall victim to summary execution on the orders of Himmler, after he was discovered to be a Soviet double agent. In the early hours of 30 June, however, Hitler was concerned with eliminating threats from within the SA, and when he arrived at the Hanselbauer Hotel in Bad Wiessee he took Ernst Röhm and the other leaders based there totally by surprise. Most were arrested, though SA

Hermann Göring

Born in 1893, and an ace fighter pilot in the First World War, Göring was a leading early member of the Nazi Party and founder of the Gestapo. He was shot in the leg while taking part in Hitler's failed military coup (the 'Beer Hall Putsch') in 1923. After being treated with morphine he became addicted to the drug for the rest of his life. Hitler named him Interior Minister of Prussia when he first came to power, giving Göring command of the largest police force in Germany. Göring promptly filled the force with committed Nazi Party members and merged the political and intelligence departments together to form the Gestapo. Originally he planned to name the force the *Geheime Polizei Amt*, ('Secret Police Office'), but the German initials GPA were too reminiscent of the Soviet secret police force, the GPU (*Gosudarstvennoye Politicheskoye Upravlenie*, or 'State Political Directorate').

It was Göring's idea to extend the fledgling force's authority throughout Germany, which he did after dismissing the Gestapo's original commander, Rudolf Diels, and taking over himself in 1934. Soon after, he relinquished control to Heinrich Himmler, and went on to become commander-in-chief of the Luftwaffe. In 1941 he became Hitler's official designated successor and deputy in all of his offices, though he was stripped of this illustrious title shortly before Hitler's suicide in 1945.

He was sentenced to death at the Nuremberg trials in 1946, but committed suicide by ingesting cyanide.

leader Edmund Heines was shot on the spot after being found in bed with an 18-year-old male troop leader.

Hitler then addressed a crowd of supporters outside his headquarters in Munich, describing his actions as a firm response to a treacherous plot to overthrow him. It was the trigger for Phase 2 of the operation, in which Gestapo death squads kicked in the doors of their unsuspecting victims and executed them. The Gestapo later furnished Hitler with a list of those they had managed to find and kill: it contained 77 names.

Vice-Chancellor Franz von Papen's inner circle were key targets. Papen had criticized Hitler in a speech at the University of Marburg two weeks earlier, and the writer of that speech was one of the first to be gunned down by the Gestapo. Edgar Julius Jung was shot in the cellar of the Gestapo headquarters then dumped in a ditch near the town of Oranienburg, just outside Berlin. Papen's secretary, Herbert von Bose, was shot at his desk in the Vice-Chancellery building itself, supposedly while resisting arrest. Another close associate of Papen, Erich Klausener, was also killed at his desk at the Ministry of Transport, and Papen himself was arrested and forced to resign. It is widely believed that Papen was due to be murdered but was saved by Göring, who believed that Papen might be more useful to the Nazis alive than dead. He was sent to Austria to be the puppet German ambassador there, preparing the way for the later annexation of that country.

Hitler's predecessor as Chancellor, Kurt von Schleicher, also received a visit from the Gestapo. He was murdered in his own home, along with his wife. His close associate Ferdinand von Bredow was tied to a chair and shot five times. Prominent former Nazi Gregor Strasser was similarly slaughtered as Hitler settled old scores with his rivals. Strasser was shot once from behind, and left to bleed to death on the floor of his prison cell, a process that reportedly took almost an hour.

It was not just high-ranking political and military figures who were murdered by the Gestapo on the Night of the Long Knives, however. Some reports suggest that in total up to 1,000 people were killed, and the most recent study names 89 certain victims. The list includes lawyers, doctors, civil servants, journalists and even a music critic. Hitler's most dangerous rival, Ernst Röhm, was handed a revolver and invited to commit suicide. When he declined to do so, he was shot in the chest at point-blank range.

By the end of the Night of the Long Knives, thanks to the ruthless efficiency of the Gestapo and SS, Hitler had total control over Germany.

Expansion and purge – at all cost

Having eliminated the political and military threats to his 'Thousand Year Reich', Hitler was now faced with the new threat of a financial meltdown in Germany. The price of the country's rapid re-armament was high, and in 1935 Germany was engulfed by an economic crisis. Hitler had prioritized importing raw materials over importing food, and as a result the queues outside shops grew longer and longer. Inflation spiralled, currency reserves collapsed and the Nazi regime's popularity sank. Over half the German population was living below the poverty line by 1935 and the Gestapo was struggling to cope with the growing dissent. Hitler desperately needed a foreign-policy triumph to distract attention away from such domestic problems.

On 7 March 1936, he ordered German troops into the demilitarized Rhineland. It was a flagrant breach of Articles 42 and 43 of the Treaty of Versailles, and Articles 1 and 2 of the Treaty of Locarno, which sought to preserve the territory as a buffer-zone between Germany and France. Hitler took the chance that France and Britain would not send troops to resist the remilitarization. The risk paid off, and German troops were welcomed as heroes when they entered Cologne for the first time since the end of the First World War.

Hitler called a referendum on the action on 29 March,

which the Gestapo helped to police. Anyone refusing to vote 'yes' was subject to intimidation and denunciation. The official turnout was close to 99 per cent, and the percentage voting in favour was similarly high.

Hitler was emboldened, and his popularity soared, but the fundamental problem of supply shortages remained. The German navy, air force and army all reported that they could not build their military capabilities without access to steel and other raw materials. Hitler called a conference on 5 November 1937 in order to outline his plan. A summary of the meeting, known as the Hossbach Memorandum, set out for the first time the expansionist policy that would soon plunge Europe into the Second World War. Germany would solve its supply problems, Hitler decided, by invading Austria and Czechoslovakia.

Himmler responded to the plan by accelerating the assimilation of the state's secret police with the SS – a dream he had long shared with Heydrich. In February 1938 Himmler decreed that the training guidelines for the Gestapo and SD should be identical. With armed conflict now inevitable, it was deemed necessary for military and state police intelligence officers to work side by side. From June 1938, all members of the security police who joined the SS were also automatically made members of the SD. The Gestapo, the SS and the SD were thus not merely separate departments that co-operated closely with one another: their guru Himmler ensured that they were all indoctrinated with the same fanatical ideology.

The Nazi policy of military expansion helped cure the issue of massive unemployment but soon created the new problem of labour shortages. To combat this, increased numbers of foreign workers were allowed into the country – many of them from Poland, where agricultural workers in particular were keen for employment. By 1938, there were almost 100,000 such Polish workers in Germany.

Discrimination against them was rife, as Poles were considered by many to be clumsy and stupid. Poles were paid less than German workers and allowed or even encouraged to work 14-hour days as opposed to the German maximum of eight hours. As a result, civil disorder between Polish workers and the local population was commonplace.

Race relations were of interest to the Gestapo as national unity was the stated key aim of the Nazi Party. Anything that undermined the sense of a single German people was considered a threat to the Reich. Foreign workers were either to be 'Germanized' or kept under strict control. There was a real fear that Poles would import communism or leftist beliefs from the east, and the Gestapo was constantly on guard for any signs of sedition.

Another concern was 'racial mixing' between Germans and Poles, and in particular between German women and Polish men. The idea of half-German and half-Polish offspring was abhorrent to the Nazis, and the Gestapo encouraged neighbours to denounce any such relationships. Women were often seized and had their hair shaved off while Gestapo officers stood by and protected those who perpetrated such acts. Though physical injury was frowned upon at this time, humiliation was not only tolerated but actively encouraged. After the outbreak of war, a Polish man convicted of sexual relations with a German woman was liable to be executed. Young Polish women who had sex with German men were treated more leniently, for the simple reason that it was incredibly common: German bosses were in a position of great power over their employees, who knew that refusing any sexual advances would lead to them losing their jobs.

Above all, the Gestapo was determined to ensure that the foreign workers remained leaderless and disorganized. They arrested or hounded any figure who appeared to threaten this goal. Or, indeed, anyone who might interfere with the larger aims of expansion and racial purity.

Anschluss

'Not as tyrants have we come, but as liberators.' This was Hitler's declaration, as German troops crossed the border into Austria on 12 March 1938.

By the time Hitler's motorcade had passed through his birthplace of Braunau, the Gestapo was already hard at work. Austrian Nazis had spent months compiling a list of 'enemies of the state', and Himmler led an advance party of SS and Gestapo officers into the Third Reich's first occupied territory ahead of the troops. The objective was to crush any resistance before it could organize; prominent anti-Nazis such as the Mayor of Vienna Richard Schmitz were rounded up and sent to Dachau concentration camp in Bavaria. Union leaders and left-wing politicians topped the wanted list, helping to ensure that when Austrians were asked to vote on whether to become part of the far-right Third Reich the over-whelming majority placed their mark in the large 'yes' circle on the ballot paper rather than daring to mark the much smaller 'no' circle.

The Gestapo soon commandeered the Hotel Metropole in Vienna as its headquarters, and in time it grew to become larger than its equivalent in Berlin, employing more than 900 staff. Countless numbers of unfortunate prisoners were taken to its soundproofed cells for inter-rogation, torture and execution during the Second World War. Many were chained backwards to the bars in their cells with their toes barely touching the floor. All were chained hand and foot during Allied bombing raids, while the Gestapo personnel cowered in the relative safety of the basement or the city's extensive catacombs. Several bombs hit the building as Vienna was pummelled towards the end of the war and the remains of the hotel were torn down to eradicate a landmark associated with terror and brutality. Today, a plaque at the site reads:

Here stood the House of the Gestapo. To those who believed in Austria it was hell. To many it was the gates to death. It sank into ruins just like the 'Thousand Year Reich'. But Austria was resurrected and with her our dead, the immortal victims.

Kristallnacht

After the annexation of Austria, the Nazi German government began to focus its attention on the question of how best to purge itself of its sizeable Jewish population. Hitler was determined to garner popularity by scapegoating the Jews for all that had gone wrong with German society. In addition, he wanted to seize Jewish property and businesses in order to shore up the precarious finances of his fledgling Reich.

His most trusted henchmen, the members of the Gestapo, were charged with driving as many Jews out of Germany and Austria as possible. They rounded up and deported some 12,000 Polish Jews across the border to Poland, giving them one night in which to pack a

Furnishings and ritual objects from the synagogue are burned in the town square, Mosbach, southern Germany, 10 November 1938.

single suitcase. Many of those forcibly removed by the Gestapo were refused entry by Polish border guards. Thousands became trapped in a makeshift refugee camp between the borders of Poland and Germany. Among them were Sendel and Riva Grynszpan, who sent a note to their son Herschel in Paris, pleading with him to help. Herschel Grynszpan responded by entering the German embassy in Paris and shooting dead a German diplomat, Ernst vom Rath.

Hitler retaliated by introducing a slew of anti-Jewish legislation, and authorizing Joseph Goebbels to make a speech which made clear that any 'spontaneous demonstrations' the German people wished to make would not be hampered. The message was received loud and clear: it was open season on Jews in the Reich. On the night of 9 November 1938, the German dictator unleashed his secret police in an act of state-sponsored terrorism that later became known as 'Crystal Night' or *Kristallnacht*. The name derives from the countless windows that were smashed during the rampage that the Gestapo co-ordinated. Shards of glass littered streets across Germany and Austria as Jewish-owned stores, homes and synagogues were attacked by angry mobs. In Vienna alone, 95 synagogues were burned – across the German Reich the figure was over 1,000. More than 7,000 Jewish businesses were damaged or destroyed. Tombstones were uprooted, sacred texts burned and statues defaced.

Many Jewish residents were also assaulted: although the official death toll was 91, several modern historians put the figure in the hundreds. In addition, some 30,000 Jews were rounded up by the Gestapo and incarcerated in concentration camps. The Nazi-employed mobs went about their brutal work while the police stood by watching, under strict instructions to protect only non-Jewish residents and foreigners. In the days after *Kristallnacht*, Jewish residents were forced to clear up the mess made by the mob, and many were obliged to scrub steps while crowds of non-Jews jeered and hurled abuse.

The attacks were widely reported by the numerous foreign correspondents based in Germany and Austria, and the first-hand accounts of the mayhem sent shock waves across Europe. It was considered a new low for a regime that the world had come to view with growing unease. Very soon, however, that unease would turn to horror. The Gestapo had only just begun.

CHAPTER TWO
THE OUTBREAK OF WAR

Terror unleashed

The Nazis' expansionist plans continued, most signif-
icantly when German forces invaded Poland in
September 1939. This resulted in Britain and France
declaring war on Germany. From the Gestapo's perspec-
tive, it also brought about the new challenge of
operating in foreign territories that were under military
occupation. Himmler hastened the integration between
the security police and the German military machine.
The Reich Security Main Office (RSHA) was founded
on 27 September 1939, bringing the security police and
SD under the same roof for the first time. Heydrich
was the natural choice as its first head. The Nazi Party's
own intelligence service now shared a physical space
with an official state service, consolidating Himmler's
power over both.

After the invasion of Poland, some 300,000 prisoners of war would be used as slave labour, and the
Gestapo's attitude to foreign workers would harden
into utter pitilessness. Before the outbreak of war,
however, the Gestapo maintained at least the veneer
of working within the judicial system when dealing
with non-Jews.

The Gleiwitz Incident

The town of Gleiwitz in Upper Silesia had been fiercely contested by Germany and Poland between the wars, before a League of Nations ruling determined it should

The radio station at Gleiwitz before it was attacked.

officially remain part of Germany. On 31 August 1939 it became the scene of a Gestapo 'false flag' operation that led to the start of the Second World War. The Nazis required a pretext for invading Poland, and utilized Gleiwitz's history of conflict to persuade the German people that the Poles intended to seize the territory by force.

The plan was hatched by Reinhard Heydrich and Heinrich Müller, the chief of the Gestapo. A small force of Gestapo agents dressed in Polish army uniforms were transported to the Gleiwitz radio station, where they broadcast a brief anti-German message in Polish. They then murdered a 43-year-old local man called Franciszek Honiok – a German who was known to be sympathetic to the Poles. He had been arrested by the Gestapo the previous day and dressed in clothing appropriate for a Polish saboteur. His corpse, complete with fresh gunshot wounds, was paraded as evidence of the fact that Poles had attacked Gleiwitz, and that one of their number had been killed by German troops.

German forces, already massed on the border with Poland, invaded the next day from the north, south and west. Hitler's great gamble was that the other European nations would not resist him militarily despite the invasion. It was a gamble that failed. Two days after the first tanks rolled across the Polish border, the United

Kingdom and France, both of whom had signed pacts with Poland, declared war on Germany.

Neither of the Allied countries was remotely ready to take on the might of the German military machine, which Hitler had so carefully prepared for the coming war. The Gestapo, meanwhile, was by now the most technologically advanced and experienced secret police force in the world. By 1939 they had the ability to monitor wireless communications and telephones. The mail service was also in its pay, and was able to steam open and reseal a suspect's mail so well that it was practically undetectable. When the Gestapo asked the mail service to monitor an individual or organization's mail, the teamwork was so efficient that the mail was delayed by just a couple of hours. The contents of any letter could be copied and sent to the local Gestapo office before the letter had even reached the intended recipient.

The secret police already had an iron grip upon the population of the Third Reich. In the coming years, as the war spread, that grip of terror would extend to cover most of Western Europe.

The Testimony of Anton Pacholegg

A great deal about the arrest of Dr Anton Pacholegg, on 2 August 1939, is shrouded in mystery. We know that he was picked up by the Gestapo on that date, and that he had been under surveillance for some time. We also know that the Gestapo believed his name to be Anton Guttenberg, and that Pacholegg used the name von Guttenberg from time to time too. Pacholegg himself later claimed that he was a patent lawyer who was picked up by the Gestapo on the Swiss border after meeting a 'business partner'. He believed the entire meeting was a ruse concocted by the Gestapo to capture him. The Gestapo files suggest that Pacholegg was accused of being a currency smuggler, but elsewhere he is referred to as a spy, and accused of committing high treason. Pacholegg stated that the Gestapo believed he was working for 'English intelligence', but that his interrogators could find no evidence to back this up.

We know nothing of what happened to Pacholegg immediately after his arrest: the next time we hear of him it is three years later, and he is languishing in the Nazi concentration camp at Dachau. He was presumably sent there in 1942 after serving a sentence handed down at trial. The Gestapo frequently picked up those who had served such sentences as soon as they were released, and sent them to the 'protective custody' of the concentration camps.

Pacholegg's story is of interest to historians because he would later testify at the Nuremberg trials and offer insight into one of the more macabre aspects of the Gestapo's operations: human medical experiments at

Dachau concentration camp. Pacholegg became the assistant to one of the most twisted SS men in history, Dr Sigmund Rascher. A close personal friend of Gestapo leader Heinrich Himmler, Rascher requested permission to experiment on those condemned to die at Dachau. Himmler incorporated the programme of human experimentation into his SS *Ahnenerbe* ('Ancestors' Heritage') institution, which was ostensibly founded to research the cultural history of the Aryan race.

The experiments at Dachau were performed by the *Ahnenerbe* offshoot 'The Institute for Military Scientific Research', presided over by Wolfram Sievers. Rascher performed the majority of the hands-on experiments, which investigated the effects of low pressure and intense cold – both subjects considered to be of potential use to the Luftwaffe. Allied aircraft were reaching heights of 12,000 m (40,000 ft) and German fighter pilots were required to follow them. At such heights gas bubbles can form in the blood vessels, resulting in potentially fatal embolisms.

It was Gestapo officers who selected which inmates would prove suitable for Rascher's sadistic experiments, which nobody outside of the SS was allowed to witness. Pacholegg later told the military tribunal at Nuremberg what he saw 'first-hand' at Dachau. There is some dispute over whether he could, in fact, have seen with his own eyes the things he later related, but it is beyond doubt that he worked very closely with Rascher and that experiments of the kind he described did indeed take place. Pacholegg stated:

I have personally seen, through the observation window of the chamber, when a prisoner inside would stand a vacuum until his lungs ruptured. Some experiments gave men such pressure in their heads that they would go mad and pull out their hair in an effort to relieve the pressure. They would tear their heads and faces with their fingers and nails in an attempt to maim themselves in their madness. They would beat the walls with their hands and head and scream in an effort to relieve pressure on their eardrums. These cases of extremes of vacuums generally ended in the death of the subject.

At least 80 victims were killed by Rascher alone at Dachau, either in low-pressure experiments or through being exposed to freezing temperatures. He also experimented with Polygal, a substance made from beets and apple pectin, to see whether it could coagulate the blood after a gunshot wound. Subjects were given a Polygal tablet, and shot through the neck or chest, or their limbs were amputated without anaesthetic. It was Pacholegg who helped give rise to one of the most infamous claims about the Nazi concentration camps, namely that the skin of dead prisoners was turned into lampshades, gloves, pocketbooks and other items after they had been

Heinrich Himmler

One of the most powerful men in Nazi Germany, Himmler was *Reichsführer* of the *Schutzstaffel* (SS) and later Chief of German Police and Minister of the Interior. He oversaw all internal and external police and security forces, including the Gestapo. It was Himmler who selected Reinhard Heydrich to head up the secret police and instructed him on how it would operate.

Born in 1900, Himmler was in a reserve battalion during the First World War and never saw action. He studied agronomy in Munich and while there met Ernst Röhm, an early member of the Nazi Party and co-founder of the paramilitary *Sturmabteilung* (SA). Himmler joined the Nazi Party in August 1923 after failing in his ambition to pursue a military career in the German army. He was involved in the failed 'Beer Hall Putsch' three months later but escaped prosecution due to insufficient evidence against him. Shortly afterwards he moved in with his parents, abandoned his Catholic faith and became ever more involved in Nazi ideology, occultism and mythology. He joined the SS and toured the country delivering speeches on behalf of Hitler and the National Socialist German Workers' Party (NSDAP).

In September 1927, Himmler outlined to Hitler a radical plan to transform the SS from a small 'personal protection' unit into an elite private army loyal to the

Nazis rather than to Germany. By January 1929 he was head of the new force and had established himself as one of Hitler's most trusted deputies. When the Nazis came to power in 1933, Himmler's SS had grown from 290 men into a force of in excess of 52,000. He was placed in charge of the country's police forces state by state until only Göring's Prussian force lay outside his control. In 1934 Göring ceded control of that force too, leaving Himmler with complete authority over the Reich's policing. Himmler placed Reinhard Heydrich in control of the secret state police, the Gestapo.

Throughout the war, Himmler was occupied with heading the SS, organizing the creation and running of concentration camps, and overseeing Heydrich's command of the Gestapo. In late 1944, with the war entering its final phase, Hitler appointed Himmler commander-in-chief of Army Group Upper Rhine (*Oberrhein*). Himmler's subsequent failure as a military commander led to him having a nervous breakdown, which destroyed Hitler's faith in him. Himmler entered into secret peace negotiations with the Allies, which resulted in him being stripped of all military ranks by a furious Hitler. After Germany's defeat, Himmler was arrested by the British while trying to escape, posing as 'Sergeant Heinrich Hitzinger'. He admitted his real identity under interrogation but committed suicide by biting on a cyanide capsule before he could be tried for war crimes.

killed. He claimed to have seen Mrs Rascher with a handbag made from human skin.

The Dachau experiments were known to be entirely contrary to international law, but Rascher's close relationship with Himmler ensured they were kept secret, and the Gestapo supplied a steady stream of prisoners to allow them to continue. Things unravelled for Rascher in March of 1944, however, when he himself became a prisoner of the Gestapo. It transpired that Rascher's large SS family of four children was not all it seemed: he and his wife had abducted the children and passed them off as their own. Himmler had used the Rascher family as a model example of Aryan breeding and was furious at being deceived. Rascher was thrown into a concentration camp at Buchenwald, and then transferred to the scene of his gruesome crimes, Dachau, when the Allied troops closed in. He was executed there by firing squad just three days before American troops liberated the camp.

Institute director Wolfram Sievers was sentenced to death on 20 August 1947 for crimes against humanity, and hanged on 2 June 1948, at Landsberg prison in Bavaria. Anton Pacholegg escaped from Dachau but was recaptured by the Gestapo. He was finally liberated in 1945, when he gave his crucial testimony to the Americans. Thereafter, he changed his name several times and moved every few years for the rest of his life, often giving conflicting stories regarding his background. This has led some to conclude that the Gestapo was right first time about Pacholegg, and that he was indeed somehow associated with the intelligence services. His story about the horrors of Dachau was corroborated by several other witnesses, however.

Throughout the war, at all of the Nazi concentration camps, the Gestapo worked hand in glove with the SS 'Death's Head Units' to guard prisoners and select those who lived or died. At Dachau, the fate of those selected to die was arguably the most horrific of all the camps in the Reich.

Johann Elser: a Long Ordeal

On 8 November 1939, a German factory worker called Johann Georg Elser planted a bomb in a beer hall in Munich, the Bürgerbräukeller. It was placed inside a speaker's rostrum due to be used by Adolf Hitler for his annual speech on the anniversary of the failed 1923 Nazi coup (the 'Beer Hall Putsch').

However, Hitler arrived earlier than scheduled and cut his speech from the customary two hours down to a single hour. He left the building at 9.07 pm, just 13 minutes before the bomb exploded. Seven members of the audience who had stayed behind were killed, and the building itself was badly damaged. The task of finding and interrogating the perpetrator fell to the Gestapo. By 11 pm the same evening, they had their man in custody at the border town of Konstanz. The next morning, Elser was transferred to Munich Gestapo headquarters.

Franz Josef Huber, head of the Gestapo in Vienna, was called in to assist in the investigation. He ordered Elser to bare his knees, which were revealed to be badly bruised as a result of all the work he had done planting the bomb in the rostrum. Now confident they had the right suspect, the Gestapo officers, led by Himmler, tortured Elser mercilessly in order to extract a confession. One eyewitness spoke of Elser groaning and bleeding profusely from multiple wounds after being beaten for hours. He finally signed a written confession on 15 November, though it was almost certainly a forgery as by then he was in no physical condition to write anything.

Despite this, Elser's ordeal was far from over. He was transferred to the Berlin Gestapo headquarters, where his mother, sister, ex-girlfriend and brother-in-law were interrogated in his presence. All maintained their innocence, and Elser continued to insist that he had acted alone, despite a further five days of agonizing torture during which the Gestapo demanded he admit to being part of a wider plot. In the end it hardly mattered: Hitler claimed that Elser was working in cahoots with the British Intelligence Service despite the official Gestapo report reluctantly concluding he was a 'lone wolf' attacker.

Elser was kept at the Berlin Gestapo headquarters until early in 1941 and was subjected to every manner of novel torture that the Gestapo could develop. He was fed salty herrings and deprived of liquids; subjected to intense heat; hypnotized and injected with methamphetamines. The only thing he revealed was how he had crafted the bomb: a design so intricate and effective that the Gestapo adopted it into their field manuals. Elser was transferred to a concentration camp and spent the rest of the war there, before being executed in April 1945 on the direct orders of Hitler. His execution was covered up and his death was blamed on an Allied air raid.

Policing far and wide

For Germany, 1940 was an extraordinary year, and the staggering success of its military machine brought the Gestapo a host of new problems to deal with. The Germans invaded and occupied Norway, Denmark, the Netherlands, Belgium, Luxembourg and France. Their ally Italy also invaded Greece. These vast new territories now had to be policed and all resistance within them crushed. The Gestapo had nowhere near enough resources to manage the task on its own. Instead, it relied on a network of informants and collaborators to feed through information about the Resistance movements of each occupied territory.

Torture and intimidation were the chief methods of 'turning' prisoners into informants. The Gestapo often threatened to arrest a suspect's entire family if they did not co-operate. Payment and favourable treatment was also used to persuade the civilian population to inform on their fellow citizens. One of the most notorious traitors of the war, Stella Kübler, was reputedly paid 300 reichsmarks for each Jew that she betrayed, for example. Nicknamed 'Blonde Poison' because of her striking good looks, Kübler gave the Gestapo information on between 600 and 3,000 Jews posing as non-Jews in Berlin. As a Jew herself, she would have been fully aware of the fate that awaited those she betrayed: indeed her own family perished at the hands of the Nazi regime.

The Gestapo also encouraged 'denunciations' from the civilian populations it controlled. Every day, citizens were told that it was their duty to inform the Gestapo of any suspicious activity they observed, or information they received. Many denounced their neighbours or work colleagues for petty or selfish reasons, hoping to ingratiate themselves with the powerful state police. Even when no information of real value was obtained by such denunciations, they helped to cultivate a state of fear and oppression that kept the population from openly discussing their hatred of the Nazis.

Hitler's hopes for a short and decisive war were

thwarted by the RAF in the skies above Britain in the summer of 1940. Losing the 'Battle of Britain' meant that Germany could not invade England as Hitler had originally intended. Morale in Germany remained high, though. The German people, and the Gestapo, were not anticipating a long and bloody conflict.

There were many, however, who would do everything in their power to make things as difficult as possible for the Nazis.

Jan Karski's Capture and Escape

At the outbreak of war, the Polish Armed Forces were hopelessly out-gunned, and without the anticipated military aid from Britain and France, defeat was inevitable. The Nazis duly took control of the country and the Polish Resistance moved underground. One of its most significant members was Jan Karski, who would later bring to the world's attention for the first time the horrors of the concentration camps and the Holocaust. In November of 1940, however, he was working as a courier between Poland and the Polish government-in-exile in Angers, France. On one such courier mission he was captured by the Gestapo while in possession of photographs of sensitive documents.

Karski's first-hand testimony of his treatment by the Gestapo was chilling, and served as a warning for all future underground operatives during the war. He

Jan Karski, captured and tortured by the Gestapo in 1940.

recounted that he was tied to a chair with Gestapo agents to his front and rear. One asked questions, which he was expected to answer without the slightest delay. Whenever he failed to do so he was struck on the jaw from behind, or beaten with piping. Even pausing to recollect details would result in fresh blows. The Gestapo knocked out all of his teeth and broke his jaw and several of his ribs. Eventually he could take it no more and slit his own wrists with a blade he had concealed in his shoe.

Karski was too valuable as an informant for the Gestapo to allow him to die, however. He was taken to a prison hospital and guarded around the clock. Despite this, the Polish Resistance managed to smuggle in a cyanide capsule for him to take if he was ever returned to the hands of his torturers. The capsule was brought in by a Resistance member dressed as a nun. She later helped Karski to escape by jumping from a second-floor window, after which he was spirited away by a group of Resistance fighters.

Due to the Gestapo's brutal reputation, anyone who was freed from their captivity was subjected to a three-month 'quarantine' period in a Resistance safe house to ensure they had not been 'turned' into a double agent. Karski's wounds healed during this period and he was able to return to Poland later in the war in order to document the horrors of the Holocaust. He also provided details of how the Gestapo handled prisoners, and to avoid such horrific treatment most Resistance members elected to carry cyanide pills on their missions throughout the rest of the war.

Battling the red army

Hitler's decision to invade the Soviet Union in 1941 fundamentally changed the focus of the war, and drew huge numbers of German troops eastwards. In their wake followed the Gestapo, and it was during this period

An Einsatzgruppe D soldier about to shoot a prisoner kneeling in front of a mass grave in Vinnitsa, Ukrainian SSR, Soviet Union, in 1942.

that many of their most heinous crimes took place. Although the *Einsatzgruppen* ('task force') death squads that operated throughout the occupied Soviet lands were nominally an SS creation, Gestapo officers worked hand-in-glove with them. The scale of the slaughter for which they were responsible is truly breathtaking, and the number of bloody incidents too numerous to list. At Babi Yar ravine in Ukraine over 33,000 people were murdered in a single operation, between 29 and 30 September 1941. Around 25,000 more were killed on two separate days at the Rumbula Forest in Latvia later the same year. This was slaughter on a scale never seen before, and though the Gestapo men were not the ones pulling the triggers they oversaw many of the most inhumane bloodbaths.

Initially the invasion of Stalin's vast homeland was a great success for Hitler, and the German forces were jubilant. By the end of the year, however, the fierce Russian winter and even fiercer Red Army resistance had slowed and then halted the German advance.

In December of 1941 Japan attacked the American naval base at Pearl Harbor, Hawaii. The United States entered the war as an ally of Britain and the Soviet Union. The Gestapo now had to adapt to the new reality of 'total war', and it was to become even more ruthless in its dealings with those who worked against it.

Maria Bruskina: a Warning to Others

On 22 June 1941, Hitler had broken his non-aggression pact with Stalin and invaded the Soviet Union. Initial progress during 'Operation Barbarossa' had been swift, with the Nazis taking vast swathes of territory in the east as they drove towards Moscow. The Soviets, caught by surprise, had appeared to be in disarray.

However, the Germans had grossly underestimated the Red Army's strength, and in the following months the invasion stalled. Hitler decided to change tack and attempt to capture the industrial centres and oil fields

Maria 'Masha' Bruskina with fellow partisans shortly before her execution in Minsk, Belarus, on 26 October 1941. A placard hung around her neck reads, in German and Russian: 'We are partisans and have shot at German troops'.

of the Caucasus in the south rather than shedding more blood seizing the Russian capital. Resistance fighters began to organize themselves within the captured territories in Belarus, Lithuania and Latvia, making them much more difficult for the Germans to hold. The Gestapo, as ever, was sent in behind the troops to terrorize the local populations and ensure that German domination of these territories continued.

One member of the Soviet Resistance handed over to the Gestapo was Maria 'Masha' Bruskina. Born into a Jewish family, she was forced to live in the Minsk ghetto in Belarus after the German army rolled into the city in July of 1941. The 17-year-old had volunteered to work as a nurse at the hospital at the Polytechnic Institute, tending to wounded members of the Red Army. In addition to this work she also helped soldiers to escape, by smuggling civilian clothing and false identity papers into the hospital. A Nazi collaborator reported what she was doing and on 14 October 1941 she was arrested by the Gestapo.

Interrogation provided no useful details regarding the Minsk underground Resistance, and so Maria was handed back to the 707th Infantry Division in order to be publicly hanged without trial. Images of her being paraded through the streets with two other members of the Resistance became famous worldwide. A placard was hung around Maria's neck stating that she was a member of the Resistance who had shot at German soldiers. Her body was left hanging for three days as a warning to others who might dare to resist the occupation. Only later when the body was cleaned did anyone learn that Masha's blonde hair was dyed as a disguise, and she remained an 'unknown partisan' until 2009 when her name was added to a memorial plaque at the execution site.

Bruskina's execution was unusual in that it was meticulously photographed and widely distributed. The Nazis soon realized that this had the opposite effect to the one they had hoped for: rather than being terrorized, those who saw the photographs instead became enraged and ever more determined to resist the occupation. Because of this, the vast majority of future executions took place in secret. The Gestapo continued to publicly execute prisoners en masse, however. Four weeks before the invasion of the Soviet Union, Himmler had created special *Einsatzgruppen* (Einsatz Groups or task forces) charged with eliminating Jews, partisans and communists, each unit headed by a member of the Gestapo or senior SD officer. The groups had complements of 400–500 men, subdivided into smaller units of *Einsatzkommandos*, who in turn were further subdivided into *Sonderkommandos* and *Teilkommandos*. Although attached to army units that determined where they worked, they took their directives directly from the RSHA in Berlin.

In the first four months of the occupation of the Soviet Union, the *Einsatzgruppen* killed hundreds of thousands of Jews, communists and members of the Resistance. The vast majority were lined up in front of deep ditches and shot in the back of the head or neck. One report writer complained bitterly about the fact that the Gestapo was hampered in its work by a lack of staff and poor working conditions:

In view of the enormous distances, the bad condition of the roads, the shortage of vehicles and petrol, and the small forces of Security Police and SD, it needs the utmost effort to be able to carry out shootings in the country. Nevertheless 41,000 Jews have been shot up to now.

'Night and Fog' Decree

'*Nacht und Nebel*' (or 'Night and Fog') was the codename given to a decree of 7 December 1941, issued by Adolf Hitler and signed by Field Marshall Wilhelm Keitel, Chief of the German Armed Forces High Command. The name stemmed from a phrase coined by Germany's celebrated writer Johann Wolfgang von Goethe, who used the term to describe clandestine operations.

The directive stated that persons captured in occupied

territories were to be brought to Germany in secret for trial by special courts, thus circumventing all international conventions governing the treatment of prisoners. Relatives and loved ones of the prisoners were given no details about the fate of the captive and were therefore left unsure where they had disappeared to, what their sentence might be, or even whether they were dead or alive. Hitler believed that the conventional systems of military and civilian justice were too cumbersome to deal effectively with resistance and sabotage activities. He therefore instructed the Gestapo to utilize 'Night and Fog' tactics to expedite interrogation, torture and execution. The decree letter specifically mentioned that the policy was designed with 'efficient intimidation' in mind, and it became one of the most feared tactics deployed by Hitler's terror police.

In practice, 'Night and Fog' was most widely used in German-occupied Western Europe, and especially common in Nazi-occupied France. After capture and interrogation by the Gestapo, 'Night and Fog' prisoners faced special kangaroo courts (*Sondergerichte*), which handed down lengthy prison sentences or, more commonly, death sentences. Those who escaped death were sent to concentration camps where they wore uniforms marked with the letters 'NN' to signify that they were '*Nacht und Nebel*' prisoners. The death rate among such prisoners was even higher than that for standard concentration camp detainees.

Later on in the war, as the Nazis' situation became increasingly desperate in the face of ever more effective resistance, Hitler issued the 'Terror and Sabotage' decree. This expanded even further on the provisions of the 'Night and Fog' decree and more often than not resulted in summary executions for all violent acts perpetrated by non-German citizens in the occupied territories. For the Gestapo it was, essentially, a 'licence to kill'.

CHAPTER THREE
RESISTANCE, RESISTANCE, RESISTANCE

The entry of the United States into the war heightened the threat to Germany and stiffened the resolve of the Nazi regime. All remaining legal or moral restraints were removed from the Gestapo. The 'Night and Fog' decree that the Gestapo now followed made the organization synonymous with midnight raids during which suspects simply disappeared without trace. Meanwhile, the grim operation of the Holocaust was accelerated. By this stage a ruthlessly efficient death machine had been engineered that was capable of killing thousands of people a day.

The Resistance movements across Europe were buoyed by the news that a powerful new ally had entered the war on their side, however. And British troops drove Rommel's forces out of North Africa, while the German advance through Russia was halted just short of Moscow. Closer to home, the Gestapo was rocked by the assassination of its leader, Reinhard Heydrich. The loss of such a charismatic head was a bitter blow for the organization, and many Gestapo officers must have felt, for the first time, that victory in the war was not assured.

The Telavåg Tragedy

Remaining neutral in the war did not spare Norway from Hitler's attention: the Scandinavian country was too strategically important to him for that. Indeed, the British had plans of their own to invade, in order to open a second front against the Germans away from France, before Hitler gave the order for his troops to cross the border on 9 April 1940. The largely unprepared Norwegians were defeated relatively swiftly, and the country would remain occupied until the capitulation of German forces in Europe in May 1945. The long occupation gave birth to widespread resistance and as a result a large contingent of Gestapo officers was stationed in Norway's major towns and cities. These Gestapo units would commit some of the most infamous crimes of the war, and in 1942 one such war crime occurred in the small Norwegian village of Telavåg.

Telavåg is located on the island of Sotra, around 39 km (24 miles) south-west of Bergen. With direct sea links to Great Britain, it was of great strategic interest to British Intelligence and to the Norwegian Resistance. The British Special Operations Executive (SOE) trained and organized Norwegian volunteers to conduct intelligence and sabotage operations under the leadership of liaison officer Captain Martin Linge. The attacks launched by Linge's Norwegian Independent

Company 1 (NOR.I.C.1) were staggeringly effective and included the operation to sabotage the heavy-water plant at Telemark. The damage caused to the Vemork Hydroelectric Plant inhibited the Nazis' development of nuclear weapons.

Linge himself was killed in 1941 during a raid on the island of Vågsøy ('Operation Archery'), but the band of special forces he established continued to be known as the *Lingekompaniet* or Linge's Company in his honour. Members of this force were at the very top of the Gestapo's most-wanted list, and when they learned that a secret smuggling route was operating out of Telavåg they were quick to investigate. The safe house harbouring them belonged to 63-year-old fisherman Lauritz Telle and his son Lars, who organized secret boat trips between Telavåg and the Shetland Islands in Britain. Fishing boats were the only vessels allowed to sail by the Germans and the crossing took some 30 hours. Telle's boats were secretly retrofitted with anti-aircraft guns, and ferried vital supplies, and Resistance fighters, back and forth between Britain and Norway. The route was known colloquially as the 'Shetland Bus'.

On 23 April, the first Gestapo agent entered Telavåg, disguised as a travelling Bible salesman, to collect information. Later, further agents in disguise arranged a 'boat trip' with Lauritz and Lars. They gave false names and addresses but established that the Telles were indeed engaged in suspicious activities, and so on 26 April the Gestapo returned, this time in the dead of night and in full uniform. The four Gestapo officers were heavily armed and had surprise on their side, but they grossly underestimated the level of resistance they would encounter. Staying with Lauritz and Lars that night were two of Linge's highly trained special forces soldiers. Arne Meldal Værum and Emil Gustav Hvaal were all too aware of the Gestapo's reputation, and were prepared to die rather than fall into the hands of the terror police. A furious gun battle developed between the Gestapo and Linge's men, during which two senior Gestapo officers were killed. Arne Værum (codenamed 'Penguin') was also killed, but Emil Hvaal (codenamed 'Anchor') managed to escape – albeit with nine separate gunshot wounds.

The surviving Gestapo officers retreated back to Bergen, where news of the incident reached the head Nazi commissioner in Norway, Josef Terboven. He immediately decided to travel to Telavåg to personally oversee the collective punishment of the village. It would be brutal, and utterly unjust, targeting every single inhabitant of Telavåg.

Lauritz Talle was taken, along with his wife and youngest child, to Gestapo headquarters in Bergen and tortured. His eldest son Lars was taken to a concentration camp near Oslo, along with 18 other men believed by the Gestapo to have been involved in the 'Shetland Bus' operation. All other men from Telavåg between the ages of 16 and 60 were sent to the Sachsenhausen concentration camp outside Berlin. They were marked for especially severe treatment and 31 of them died in the camp. The women and children were taken to a prisoners' camp a few hours from Bergen. Commissioner Terboven then ordered the total destruction of Telavåg, and that its name be removed from all maps. Every home was rigged with dynamite and blown to pieces. The village was so utterly obliterated that not even the wells remained.

Gerhard Flesch

A fanatical Nazi whose last words before a firing squad were '*Heil Hitler!*', Gerhard Flesch headed the Gestapo in Norway. In this role he executed countless members of the Norwegian Resistance, often without trial. He was notorious for torturing captives in order to extract information from them, and was also chief of the Falstad concentration camp near Trondheim. He fled from there after the war (with a gold bar in his luggage), but was caught and tried for war crimes in 1946. His guilt, and the resultant death sentence, were never in doubt and he was executed in 1948.

Emil Hvaal was captured and transported to a concentration camp to be executed. His wife Kamilla was allowed to visit him in hospital before his transportation. Her parting words to him were '*Vær Norsk*', which translate as 'Be Norwegian'.

The Daring Assassination of Reinhard Heydrich

One million reichsmarks was a vast sum of money in 1942, and in the end it was too tempting an offer for

Rows of murdered civilians from the village of Lidice near Prague, Czechoslovakia, June 1942.

Karel Čurda to resist. The Nazis offered the reward in return for information that would lead to the arrest of those responsible for the most audacious and high-profile assassination of the Second World War, that of Reinhard Heydrich, the head of the Gestapo, which took place in the Czechoslovak capital, Prague. Čurda, a Czech, was a member of the sabotage group 'Out Distance' and was facing intensive interrogation by Gestapo officers, who believed he was involved in the Heydrich assassination plot. He elected to betray his underground comrades and pocket the cash rather than face brutal torture at the hands of his Gestapo handlers. Indeed, under his new identity of 'Karl Jerhot' he became a valuable Gestapo spy for the rest of the war, after which he was captured and hanged for treason.

Čurda was the break the Gestapo were desperate for in their investigation into Heydrich's murder. The pressure from Hitler to find and punish those responsible was intense. At the time of his assassination, Heydrich was not only head of the Gestapo but also chief of the Reich Security Main Office and Protector of Bohemia and Moravia. The slaying of such a high-ranking Nazi official sent shock waves through Germany. Until 1942 the occupied Czech lands had offered little in the way of visible resistance to the Nazis and had produced valuable military material for the Third Reich. The

'Whip and Sugar' policy instigated by Heydrich, in which rations were increased to dissuade resistance, with the threat of them being reduced in the event of trouble, seemed to be working. Heydrich had arrested some 5,000 anti-Nazi partisans and so many of them ended up on the scaffold that he was nicknamed the 'Hangman'.

'Operation Anthropoid', as the assassination was codenamed, had been organized by the British Special Operations Executive with the approval of the Czechoslovak government-in-exile. It was designed for maximum effect in terms of boosting morale and inspiring further resistance across occupied Nazi Europe. Jozef Gabčík and Jan Kubiš were airlifted from the United Kingdom into Czechoslovakia, along with seven soldiers from Czechoslovakia's army-in-exile. On 27 May 1942, they waited at a tram stop near a tight curve on a road in Prague, known to be on Heydrich's daily commute from his home in Panenské Břežany to Prague Castle. As Heydrich's open-topped Mercedes 320 Convertible B reached the spot, Gabčík stepped out in front of it and opened fire with his British Sten sub-machine gun. Nothing happened. The gun jammed. Heydrich, fatally, ordered his driver to stop the car rather than speeding away.

Kubiš grabbed a grenade from his briefcase and hurled

it at the car. The highly sensitive impact fuse prepared by the British SOE caused the grenade to explode as soon as it struck the rear wheel and bumper of the car. The car, unlike most official Nazi vehicles, was not armour-plated. Shrapnel tore through Heydrich's body, but he managed to draw his pistol and trade fire with the assassins. As they fled, Heydrich and his driver pursued them, until Heydrich was forced to stagger back to the car, bleeding heavily. His driver continued to chase Gabčík until two revolver rounds to his leg forced him to let the assassin go. Gabčík and Kubiš escaped largely unhurt, but were convinced their attack had failed. In fact, however, Heydrich's shrapnel wounds were severe and his driver had suffered serious gunshot injuries to the leg.

Despite excellent medical treatment, Heydrich died of his wounds on 4 June. It was probably horsehair from the car's upholstery that festered in his wound to cause a fatal infection. He lay in state for two days before his coffin, draped in swastika flags, was taken on a tour past famous Nazi landmarks on its way to Berlin's Invaliden cemetery. By then a state of emergency had been declared in Czechoslovakia and the huge reward for information had been offered. Hitler ordered the Gestapo to 'wade in blood' throughout Bohemia in order to capture the culprits, and the secret police needed no further encouragement. Hitler's original plan was the simple mass murder of thousands of Czech civilians, but the area was vital to the Reich's industrial output and wiser heads suggested the labour force was too important to lose.

Then came the arrest and betrayal of Karel Čurda. Before paying him the bounty, the Gestapo made sure to extract from him the name of every associate he knew in Czechoslovakia. It was a disaster for the partisans. Already hundreds of suspects had been arrested throughout the country, and now the Gestapo had a long list of names and addresses of confirmed conspirators. Those they had already arrested who were not on that list were usually executed or transported to concentration camps anyway: the Gestapo simply went after anyone they considered 'suspicious'. This included eight men and seven women from the Horak families in Lidice, a favourite drop-point for Resistance paratroopers. They were arrested on 28 May, and the inhabitants of Lidice doubtless imagined that the Gestapo would leave the village alone after that. They were tragically mistaken.

On the evening of 9 June, the Gestapo returned with reinforcements. This time, the entire village was sealed off and Gestapo officers went from house to house, ordering everyone out into the street in their night-clothes. As they watched, their homes were torn apart by Gestapo officers looking for anything incriminating. In total almost 200 men were marched out of the village to the farm owned by the Horak family. There, they were lined up, and mattresses were placed against the walls to prevent ricochets. As Nazi film cameras rolled, in groups of five or ten, all of the men were shot. In addition, 52 women were killed, and all other inhabitants of the village were transported to a concentration camp. The buildings of Lidice were soaked with petrol and then burnt to the ground. Bulldozers and dynamite were used to destroy the remaining walls and uproot trees. It is said that even a stream that once flowed through the village was diverted.

Jewish prisoners were bussed in from a concentration camp to dig a mass grave for the executed men. The children of Lidice fared hardly any better than the adults: the vast majority were handed over to the Gestapo office in Łódź, Poland, from where they were taken to Chelmno concentration camp and gassed. Others died in the brutally austere German orphanages. Of the 101 who were taken away from their homes, just 17 made it back alive to Lidice.

None of those living in Lidice had anything to do with 'Operation Anthropoid'. However, the Gestapo's investigation revealed that several inhabitants from the village of Ležáky did help the assassins. A radio set was secretly hidden there. On 24 June, every man and woman in the village was shot. In total, 33 were executed, with a further 13 children taken away, and the village itself was levelled.

The two assailants themselves hid in safe houses before taking refuge in Karel Boromejsky church in Prague. When Karel Čurda betrayed his comrades to the Gestapo, the net closed in almost immediately. A raid on the home of the Moravec family in Žižkov occurred on 17 June. Marie Moravec and her son Ata were key members of the Resistance, and Marie chose to bite upon a cyanide capsule rather than face a Gestapo interrogation. Her son Ata was tortured, made drunk on brandy and then shown his mother's severed head in a fish tank in order to get him to talk. It was the Gestapo's threat to kill his entirely innocent father that finally persuaded him to give his tormentors the information they wanted.

Though the Gestapo was desperate to take the two assassins alive, ultimately Gabčík and Kubiš chose to fight to the death. A two-hour gun battle at the church ended with Kubiš dying from his wounds and Gabčík committing suicide, along with three other partisans.

In total the number killed by the Gestapo in revenge for the assassination of their leader is estimated at around 1,300.

The Oslo Mosquito Raid

When the British learned that the Nazi-appointed fascist Norwegian leader Vidkun Quisling had organized a rally for 25 September 1942, they decided to launch a raid on that date in order to boost the morale of the Resistance. The most loathed symbol of Nazi power was the Gestapo headquarters, based at the Victoria Terrasse building in Oslo. The Royal Air Force used the raid to announce to the British public a new aeroplane: the de Havilland Mosquito. It was a fast fighter-bomber that would subsequently take part in some of the RAF's most famous raids and garner the nickname the 'Wooden Wonder'.

Four Mosquitoes took part in the attack, which involved a round trip of some 1,800 km (1,100 miles). One was shot down by the Luftwaffe's Focke-Wulf Fw 190 fighters, but the other three returned safely and at least four bombs smashed through the Gestapo headquarters. Three of them penetrated the building and exited through the rear wall before exploding. The fourth failed to detonate. The Gestapo building was thus damaged rather than destroyed as intended, and several surrounding civilian residences bore the brunt of the damage. The Norwegian government-in-exile, which had not been informed of the raid in advance, protested when news of 80 civilian deaths reached them.

Gestapo operations in Norway were, however, badly disrupted by the attack, and it further weakened the position of Quisling, whose star was already in the descendent in Hitler's eyes. Fascists attending Quisling's rally had to run for their lives as the Mosquitoes hurtled across the skies of Oslo as low as 13 m (40 ft). The British and Norwegian public received a major boost to morale as a result of such a high-profile raid: 'Nazis Stung by Mosquitoes' read the headline on the front page of *The Times*.

The Gestapo retained an iron grip on the population for the remainder of the war, despite fierce resistance from bands of Norwegian underground fighters. The success of the Gestapo in Norway was due in no small part to active collaboration from certain well-connected locals. These undercover collaborators posed as anti-Nazi civilians and engaged others in conversation on buses and in cafés. Any signs of sedition were reported back to their Gestapo superiors. One of the most active Gestapo units was *Sonderabteilung Lola*, led by ex-Norwegian army truck driver Henry Rinnan. He infiltrated various Resistance groups and personally tortured and murdered those he later arrested. It is believed more than 80 people died at the hands of *Sonderabteilung Lola*.

Rinnan was executed after the war, along with another

notorious collaborator and Gestapo agent, Siegfried Fehmer. Fehmer was infamous for setting his pet German shepherd dog on his prisoners. He was captured after the war when British Military Police posted a round-the-clock watch on the dog, banking on the fact that Fehmer would attempt to collect it before fleeing. He did so, and was put in front of a firing squad on 16 March 1948.

The Red Orchestra Spy Ring

'The Red Orchestra' (*Die Rote Kapelle*) was one of the most successful spy rings of the Second World War, operating throughout Nazi-occupied Western Europe and in the very heart of Hitler's Third Reich, Berlin. Although ostensibly a Soviet-run operation, its agents included Poles, Frenchmen and women, Germans and Brits. The Nazis were aware that such a ring was operating as early as June 1941, as several intercepted radio messages appeared to share the same call signs and ciphers. The Germans termed enemy radio operators 'pianists', after the Soviet term 'musicians', which is where the name 'Red Orchestra' stemmed from. However, it took until December 1942 for the Gestapo to finally track down its key members. When they did smash the ring, their response was typically brutal.

Leopold Trepper was the heart of the operation. A

Leopold Trepper, organizer of the Red Orchestra spy ring, photographed in 1974.

Soviet military intelligence service officer, he established a small espionage ring in 1939 in Brussels, posing as the proprietor of a firm selling raincoats. Following the fall of Belgium, he moved to Paris in May 1940 and set up further 'cover firms' there. Gradually Trepper's spy ring expanded, and at the time of its discovery the Red Orchestra was comprised of three main branches: the Trepper network in France, Belgium and Holland, the 'Schulze-Boysen' network in Berlin and the 'Lucy Ring' operating out of neutral Switzerland. Harro Schulze-Boysen was an intelligence officer assigned to the German Air Ministry and thus had access to extraordinarily sensitive information that, when leaked, caused significant damage to Nazi operations. The Lucy Ring included Lieutenant General Fritz Theile, a senior *Wehrmacht* communications branch officer, and Colonel Rudolf Christoph Freiherr von Gersdorff, an Army Group intelligence officer on the Eastern Front. The Nazis could hardly fail to notice that top-secret information kept falling into enemy hands, and they made finding the source of the leaks a top priority for the Gestapo.

The agents of the Red Orchestra, however, were highly skilled and extremely diligent in covering their tracks. Teams of radio trackers who scoured the streets of Berlin every night looking to pin down the source of the spies' transmissions were thwarted time and time again. The

73

'pianists' who transmitted via secret receivers constantly changed their locations, call-signs and broadcast wavelengths.

Things began to unravel for the Red Orchestra in spring 1942, when the Gestapo arrested over 600 people in Germany, France and Belgium. Many were innocent but some were major figures within the espionage network. The Gestapo's brutal torture techniques (known officially as 'intensified interrogation') broke the resistance of some, and they began to talk. One lead led inexorably to another, and eventually Trepper himself was arrested on 5 December 1942 in Paris. He agreed to become a double agent for the Germans and began to transmit disinformation under the close scrutiny of his handlers. However, Trepper managed to escape in September 1943 and survived the war after being sheltered by the French Resistance. It is widely believed that he was able to tip off the Soviets by deliberately broadcasting mistakes in the messages he sent under duress.

The vast majority of the Red Orchestra did not share Trepper's happy ending. Suzanne Spaak, one of Trepper's most important agents, was executed at Fresnes Prison, south of Paris, just 13 days before the liberation of the French capital after years of torture and mistreatment. Mildred Harnack, a lecturer before the war and crucial member of the Schulze-Boysen network during it, was given a sentence of six years' hard labour. Hitler, enraged in the wake of the German defeat at Stalingrad, ordered a retrial and this time she received the same sentence as her husband Arvid: death. Harro Schulze-Boysen himself was executed in December 1942, along with his wife and co-conspirator Libertas.

In total, more than 50 of the group's members were murdered. During the period in which it operated, however, the Red Orchestra did huge damage to the Nazi war effort. By the time it was discovered and destroyed by the Gestapo, the tide of the war had turned against the Nazis. An increasingly paranoid Adolf Hitler would blame all of his woes on betrayal, and turn ever more frequently to his trusted secret police to liquidate the traitors. The Gestapo's reign of terror had yet to reach its peak.

'Operation Freshman'

By late 1942, the German atomic weapons programme was believed to be on the brink of successfully creating a nuclear reactor. One of the key problems they still had to overcome was creating enough deuterium-enriched 'heavy water' to allow a reactor to operate. The heavy water was produced at the Vemork Hydroelectrical plant in Telemark, Norway. British commandos were dispatched to destroy it on 19 November 1942. It was the first British attack to utilize gliders, and from the outset things went disastrously wrong. Both of the gliders used in the assault crash-landed, resulting in the deaths of 15 servicemen. All of the remaining commandos were left injured and far from help, and were soon arrested by the Gestapo.

Adolf Hitler had issued his infamous 'Commando Order' a month earlier, which stated that all commando troops were to be killed immediately upon capture. Three of the four surviving crew from the first glider were tortured by the Gestapo before being murdered by having air injected into their bloodstreams. The fourth was shot in the back of the head the following day. The surviving crew from the second glider fared no better. Five uninjured men were sent to Grini concentration camp where they were held until January 1943. Gestapo agents then marched them out into woods and shot them. The remaining survivors were shot within a few hours of being captured.

The Gestapo flooded the area with armed officers and arrested over 21 local people for questioning. However, the team of Norwegian saboteurs with whom the British had been due to rendezvous managed to slip away. They would return to the same target later in the war, with far greater success.

CHAPTER FOUR
THE GROWING CHALLENGE

On 2 February 1943, news of the surrender of the German 6th Army at Stalingrad sent shock waves through the German Reich, and shattered the myth of German military invincibility. The Gestapo had benefited from the same aura of omnipotence, and now found its authority being openly challenged by the German population for the first time. Less than a month after the Stalingrad surrender, the Gestapo began a massive operation to round up the almost 9,000 Jews in Berlin who were spouses in or children of 'mixed marriages'. Designated 'exempted Jews', they had been spared deportation to concentration or forced-labour camps thus far. On 27 February 1943, almost 2,000 of them were transported to the Jewish community building at Rosenstrasse 2–4.

As word of the operation spread, something extraordinary began to happen: the spouses, siblings and friends of those captured by the Gestapo gathered on the streets outside the building. Mostly women, they refused to leave until given assurances that their loved ones were not going to be deported. A crowd of 200 stood in the freezing temperatures and openly defied repeated orders to disperse. It was an unparalleled protest and soon made headline news across the world. Never before had the German people protested on behalf of Jews, and the Gestapo simply did not know how to react.

In the end, all but 25 of the 2,000 prisoners were released – though the vast majority were quietly re-arrested once the protest had died down. The German authorities were worried that the German public's morale was collapsing and they feared public unrest if they cracked down too hard on their own citizens. The British RAF and US Eighth Air Force began round-the-clock bombing of German cities later the same year, further damaging morale. Allied forces landed in Sicily, and Italy soon surrendered, drawing German forces south to defend Rome in place of the Italian army.

Until this point the Gestapo had concerned itself mainly with foreign spies and Resistance fighters. From 1943 onwards they also had to deal with an increasing level of resistance to the war from within the Reich itself.

The White Rose Movement

The year 1943 began badly for the Germans on the Eastern Front, with a massive counter-attack by the Soviets at Stalingrad on 10 January. The Germans were forced to surrender on 2 February, the first major defeat for a German army at the hands of the supposedly genetically inferior Red Army. By now some of the German public were aware of the mass execution of Jews in concentration camps, with the British Foreign Secretary having pledged in the House of Commons to bring those responsible to justice. A stream of Germans who had witnessed the horrors of the war on the Eastern Front flooded back to the Fatherland. Many of them now realized the madness and brutality of the Nazi regime and dedicated themselves to destroying it. In the summer of 1942, several students from the University of Munich formed themselves into a Resistance group called the 'White Rose Movement'.

The movement was non-violent and targeted the German intelligentsia, mailing leaflets directly to those in a position of power or influence and leaving pamphlets in public places for the general public to find. Most were written by Alexander Schmorell, an Eastern Orthodox Christian who had both German and Russian ancestry. Schmorell had served as a combat medical assistant in the Russian campaign and was one of the founders of the White Rose, alongside fellow University of Munich alumnus Hans Scholl and another medical student, Willi Graf. In January 1943 the group produced 9,000 anti-Nazi leaflets using a hand-operated duplicating machine and a network of couriers operating in cities throughout Germany. This print run, exhorting the German people to support the Resistance and warning them that defeat was inevitable, caused a sensation. The search for the source of the propaganda became the Gestapo's top priority.

The scrawling of the slogans 'Freedom' and 'Down with Hitler!' on the walls of Munich University buildings gave the Gestapo the first clue that students of the institution might be involved. But it was when Hans Scholl went further and personally left leaflets in the lecture rooms of the university that things began to unravel for the White Rose. A maintenance man at the university observed Hans and his sister Sophie hurling leaflets from a top-floor window, and reported them to the authorities. They were interrogated by Robert Mohr, the head of the Gestapo special commission established to search for the White Rose agitators. After initially claiming to be innocent, both siblings admitted their involvement on being presented with incontrovertible evidence. However, they continued to insist they were the only ones involved in the production of the leaflets. The two, along with co-conspirator Christoph Probst, were charged with treason.

What followed was a Nazi show-trial during which prosecutor Roland Freisler, the Gestapo's favourite judge, berated the conspirators for their ingratitude towards the Fatherland. The sentences were never in doubt, and all three were duly ordered to be beheaded. In a particularly ruthless gesture, the executions were carried out the very same day. In due course a total of seven members of the White Rose group were executed, and more than a dozen more were imprisoned. Alexander Schmorell was sent to the guillotine after a second show-trial, alongside fellow White Rose member Kurt Huber. Willi Graf was beheaded on 12 October 1943 after six months' imprisonment and torture by Gestapo

The 'Manifesto of the Students of Munich' and accompanying explanation. Thousands of copies of this pamphlet were dropped over Germany by the British Royal Air Force in 1943.

interrogators. He revealed no information of value. Hundreds of suspected supporters and sympathizers were arrested and interrogated by the Gestapo, some for simply being in possession of White Rose leaflets. The final leaflet produced by the White Rose was smuggled out of Germany and reprinted by the British as the propaganda leaflet 'Manifesto of the Students of Munich'. Millions of copies of the manifesto were dropped over Germany by Allied bombers, and today the group are regarded in Germany as national heroes.

Roland Freisler

Freisler was the judge appointed by the Nazis to preside over the 'People's Court', where many 'political crimes' prosecuted by the Gestapo were heard. It was essentially a kangaroo court, and no defendant brought before Freisler could expect a fair trial. Famous for shouting abuse at those brought before him, Freisler happily handed down death sentences for any crimes that he considered harmed the ability of the Nazi regime to protect itself. He was killed in 1945 when American bombers scored a direct hit on the courtroom while Freisler was presiding there.

Sophie Scholl went to the guillotine with the following words:

Such a fine, sunny day, and I have to go, but what does my death matter, if through us, thousands of people are awakened and stirred to action?

The Return of Dietrich Bonhoeffer

Though the Gestapo generally targeted political dissidents and artistic 'degenerates', it also had a department responsible for arresting 'religious opponents'. One of this department's most famous victims was arrested in 1943. Dietrich Bonhoeffer was picked up by the Gestapo's 'IV B' department, which dealt with regional policy, alongside 'IV A', which handled subjects hostile to the state, including 'religious opponents'. He was initially imprisoned at Tegel military prison in Berlin. A well-known and popular Lutheran pastor, he was an outspoken critic of the Nazi regime and its policy of genocide against the Jews. He was also a prominent member of the *Abwehr*, the German military intelligence organization that was a hotbed of anti-Hitler sentiment during the war.

Bonhoeffer had been under surveillance by the Gestapo since 1941, when he was forbidden to publish any further writings or make radio broadcasts that were critical of Hitler. Bonhoeffer had warned of the dangers of the Nazi regime ever since its rise to power

Dietrich Bonhoeffer, German theologian, arrested by the Gestapo in 1943.

in 1933, and in one message urged the church not to 'bandage the victims under the wheel, but jam the spoke in the wheel itself'. He resisted the Nazification of the German Evangelical Church and asserted the supremacy of Christ over the Führer as head of the church. In autumn 1933, Bonhoeffer left Germany for England and then Switzerland; he returned to Germany in 1935. The church he had helped to found (the 'Confessing Church') was shut down by the Gestapo in 1937, and 27 pastors associated with Bonhoeffer were arrested. Despite this, Bonhoeffer continued to offer services in East German villages, continually moving and lodging with sympathetic friends. In 1938, the Gestapo officially banned him from Berlin, and the following year Bonhoeffer left for the safety of America. Once there, however, he soon came to the conclusion:

I will have no right to participate in the reconstruction of Christian life in Germany after the war if I do not share the trials of this time with my people.

Returning to Germany now that war had broken out was incredibly risky, but Bonhoeffer believed he had to follow his conscience. From the moment he arrived back he was harassed by Gestapo officers and ordered to report to them regularly. Despite their constant attention, Bonhoeffer became a courier for the German Resistance, travelling across Europe under the cover of being an *Abwehr* intelligence officer. Almost inevitably, given the Gestapo's long-held mistrust of him, he was arrested, interrogated and imprisoned in April 1943.

Bonhoeffer was detained for 18 months, ostensibly awaiting trial, though in reality it suited the Gestapo simply to shut him away where he could do little harm. Many of his prison guards were sympathetic to him and one even offered to help him escape, but Bonhoeffer refused on the grounds that the Gestapo would then target his family instead. Everything changed in 1944, when the failed plot to assassinate Adolf Hitler on 20 July led to a massive Gestapo investigation into the *Abwehr*. Bonhoeffer was discovered to have been involved in the *Abwehr*'s anti-Nazi conspiracy and he was immediately transferred to the Gestapo's high-security prison at the Reich Security Main Office. After interrogation there, he was transported in secret to Flossenbürg concentration camp.

On 4 April 1945, Hitler read the diaries of the head of the *Abwehr*, Admiral Wilhelm Canaris. Enraged by their treacherous contents, he ordered the immediate execution of all those involved in the *Abwehr* conspiracy, including Bonhoeffer. He was hanged just two weeks before United States forces liberated the concentration camp. Many other *Abwehr* members and Resistance fighters were hanged alongside him, as the Gestapo liquidated as many witnesses to their own barbarity as possible before the Allied forces closed in.

Jean Moulin: The Man Who Knew Everything

France had one of the best-organized Resistance movements of the war, the military wing of which was the
Armée Secrète ('Secret Army') led by General Charles
Delestraint. They were given significant support from
the British just across the Channel, who provided arms,
training and intelligence throughout the Nazi occupation. The threat of the French Resistance was so great
that one of the Gestapo's most infamous leaders was

French Resistance member Jean Moulin, circa 1940.

stationed in Vichy France to counter it. Klaus Barbie, the 'Butcher of Lyon', would play a key role in one of the most infamous arrests of the war, that of French national hero Jean Moulin in 1943.

The story really began with the arrest in Paris of Delestraint, though many believe that another arrest prior to this actually led to the Resistance being betrayed. It is alleged that a Resistance member by the name of René Hardy was captured and tortured by Barbie, and it was he who gave them Delestraint's name. Regardless of who betrayed Delestraint, his arrest sent shock waves through the underground Resistance. It was a major coup for Barbie's Gestapo men and a terrible blow to the anti-Nazi forces led by Moulin. The young one-time *préfet* (state representative) had been chosen by France's leader-in-exile Charles de Gaulle to unify the piecemeal Resistance in occupied France and had discharged his mission brilliantly to date. He had already been arrested once by the Germans in 1940, and shortly afterwards attempted to commit suicide by slitting his throat. Ever since that unsuccessful attempt he had worn a trademark scarf around his throat to cover the scar. He was, in June 1943, one of the most-wanted men in Nazi-occupied France.

Moulin hastily organized a conference of key Resistance leaders in a doctor's house in Caluire, a suburb of the city of Lyon. His great genius lay in holding together the disparate forces of the Resistance, and he was desperate that all of the main factions should agree upon a successor to Delestraint. René Hardy was one of those in attendance, and is frequently cited as the man who betrayed the meeting's location to the Gestapo. Some, however, claim that Hardy was simply careless and the Gestapo tailed him to the meeting. Others suggest that Moulin was betrayed by rogue communists. What is not in dispute is that the Gestapo raided the house and arrested several high-ranking members of the Resistance, including its head, Jean Moulin. Hardy escaped the raid, which fuelled suspicions that he had been 'turned' by the Gestapo after his earlier arrest.

Part of the reason that we know what happened next is due to the twisted mind of Moulin's principal tormentor, Klaus Barbie. When he had finished torturing Moulin he placed his battered half-dead body on display as a warning to the other suspects. If they refused to talk, he told them, this is what would become of them. Moulin was laid out on a chaise longue in Barbie's office like a gruesome, living museum exhibit of Nazi brutality. Aware that the man they had captured was the head of the French Resistance and could thus name all senior figures involved in the conspiracy, Barbie personally tortured Moulin for three straight weeks. Hot needles were shoved under his fingernails, and his fingers were forced between the hinges of a door, which was slammed shut repeatedly until Moulin's knuckles broke. Handcuffs were tightened with screws until they tore through his flesh and broke the bones beneath. He was routinely whipped and beaten, until the skin hung from his flesh in strips. His face was so badly beaten that even his friends could barely recognize him.

Too badly injured even to talk any more, Moulin was given a piece of paper by Barbie and ordered to write down the names of his co-conspirators. He responded by drawing a mocking caricature of his torturer. Eventually, after more remorseless torture, the head of the French Resistance slipped into a coma. He had not revealed a single detail of use to the Gestapo. Barbie ordered him to be taken to Berlin, via Paris. Moulin died en route – either from his injuries, or from suicide. As a result of his refusal to betray his colleagues, the French Resistance survived as an effective organization and would later play a crucial role in preventing the Nazis from re-inforcing their positions on D-Day. The Allies successfully gained a foothold on the beaches of northern France, and from there marched all the way to Berlin. The importance of Moulin's heroic silence cannot be overstated.

Moulin's sister later summed up his story with the following words:

Klaus Barbie

Nikolaus 'Klaus' Barbie, the infamous 'Butcher of Lyon', personally tortured suspected members of the French Resistance while working for the Gestapo in France. He was born in 1913 in Godesberg, now part of Bonn. He originally wanted to study theology but became actively involved in the Nazi Party after being drafted into its labour service while he was temporarily unemployed. He rose through the ranks of the security service of the *Schutzstaffel* (SS) and the *Sicherheitsdienst* (SD), and was posted to Amsterdam after the German conquest of the Netherlands.

In November 1942 Barbie was sent to Lyon to head the local Gestapo at the Hôtel Terminus. The name Barbie and the Gestapo's French address would become synonymous with many of the cruellest and most sadistic of the Gestapo's war crimes. Historians estimate that Barbie was involved in the deaths of up to 14,000 people. One witness described her father being beaten, skinned alive and then plunged head-first into a bucket of ammonia. In return, the Nazi regime awarded Barbie the 'First Class Iron Cross with Swords' for his work in quelling the French Resistance.

After the war, the French sentenced Barbie to death *in absentia*, but by then he was working as an agent for the United States, who helped him flee to Bolivia. There he worked for a number of Bolivian dictators and

senior generals, and drew a salary from the West German intelligence agency, the BND. He was also alleged to have played a major role in the assassination of Che Guevara in 1967.

He was finally extradited to France in 1984, and sentenced to life imprisonment in 1987. He died of cancer in a Lyon prison four years later.

His part was played, and his ordeal began. Jeered at, savagely beaten, his head bleeding, his internal organs ruptured, he attained the limits of human suffering without betraying a single secret; he who knew everything.

The Polish 'War Within a War'

Resistance organizations elsewhere in Europe were of secondary importance to the overall Allied war effort, with one exception: Poland. The Polish Underground State, and its armed wing, the Home Army (*Armia Krajowa*), were crucial suppliers of intelligence to the British, and their efforts in sabotaging and harassing German forces in the East were vital to the Soviets. Several German divisions were tied down in fighting the Polish threat, and the Allies were alerted to the threats of the V-1 and V-2 flying bombs and rockets by the Poles. Perhaps inevitably, then, the Gestapo's presence in Poland was significant, and anyone suspected of being a member of the Polish Underground could expect no mercy at its hands.

In retaliation for the brutal tactics of the Gestapo, the Polish Underground tracked down and assassinated known collaborators and agents of the Gestapo. One of the most prominent of these was the actor and stage performer Igo Sym. Before the war he had acted alongside major stars such as Marlene Dietrich. When the war broke out he settled in Warsaw, where he became one of the most high-profile figures to embrace the occupying Nazi regime. In late 1939 he became a Gestapo agent, and helped set a trap that caught several prominent members of the Polish Resistance. The Underground took their revenge in 1941, when they assassinated Sym at his Warsaw apartment, posing as delivery men.

The Gestapo's response was a 'Palmiry Massacre'. Throughout the war, these mass executions in the Kampinos Forest near the village of Palmiry, north-west of Warsaw, were used to intimidate the local population and dissuade them from helping the Resistance. It is believed that between 1939 and July 1941 some 1,700 Poles were taken into the forest glades and shot. The majority were Jews and what the Germans considered the Polish 'intelligentsia'.

Often, when the Gestapo wanted to track down a particularly high-value target, they would take hostages from the general population and threaten to murder them unless the target they sought was brought to them. The *łapanka* (round-up) of random civilians was a favourite terror tactic of the Gestapo across Europe, but was especially prevalent in Poland – and in Warsaw in particular. This is what happened in the case of the assassination of Igo Sym. A total of 21 prisoners, including two professors from the University of Warsaw, were shot when no one came forward with the names of the assassins. It was, in truth, nothing out of the ordinary by the Gestapo's standards: between 1942 and 1944, the number of victims executed was estimated to be around 400 per day. Some 37,000 were killed during the war at the local Gestapo-run Pawiak prison alone.

The struggle between the Gestapo and the Polish Underground State had thus become a 'war within a war' in Warsaw by 1943. Both sides considered it a battle to the death. The commander of the Polish Home Army, Stefan Rowecki, was the Gestapo's most high-value target of all. A legendary Polish general who had fought the Nazis ever since they first invaded, he inspired fanatical loyalty and organized his Underground army into a ruthlessly efficient force of resistance. Unbeknownst to Rowecki, however, the Gestapo had infiltrated his organization with double agents of its own.

Ludwik Kalkstein is perhaps the most notorious Polish traitor of all time, betraying his fellow countrymen not only to the occupying Nazis during the Second World War, but to the occupying Soviet forces after the end of the war too. Turned by the Gestapo after intensive interrogation in 1942, Kalkstein led them to Rowecki, who was immediately arrested and turned over to the Gestapo's most senior interrogators. Himmler himself was involved in questioning Rowecki, and when he departed he ordered progress reports on Rowecki's questioning to be delivered to him every evening. The Nazis had by now suffered serious defeats at the hands of the Red Army and were desperate to try to persuade the Polish Resistance to side with them against the communists. They believed that if they could turn Rowecki over to their cause then his influence would win over the rest of the Polish Resistance. For this reason, Rowecki escaped the kind of brutal torture suffered by Jean Moulin and countless other Gestapo prisoners.

Despite intensive questioning lasting many weeks, and offers of hugely favourable treatment if he changed sides, Rowecki refused to either collaborate with the Germans or provide them with any information. He was eventually taken to Sachsenhausen concentration camp while the senior Nazi leadership decided how best to deal with him. The answer came after the Warsaw Uprising in August 1944, when Polish Jews revolted with the assistance of the Polish Home Army. In reprisal, Rowecki was executed, on the direct orders of Himmler.

Rowecki's arrest and subsequent death was a hammer blow for the Polish Resistance, but things were to get worse. The commander of the National Armed Forces (NSZ) was also captured by the Gestapo in the same period. Colonel Ignacy Oziewicz had been negotiating with the leaders of the Home Army in order to form a coalition between the two Resistance forces. He was sent to Auschwitz but managed to survive the war. Just a couple of weeks after the arrest of these two senior Resistance figures, the prime minister of the Polish government-in-exile, General Władysław Sikorski, was also killed. A plane carrying Sikorski crashed shortly after take-off from the British-controlled territory of Gibraltar. Officially ruled an accident by investigators, many conspiracy theories have suggested he was murdered, either by Polish rivals or by the British or Soviets. Whatever the truth, the Polish Resistance had lost three of its most senior figures within the space of a month, and the Gestapo had restored its iron grip on the Polish population.

Destruction of the Prosper Network

The British Special Operations Executive's largest Resistance network in occupied France was the 'Physician-Prosper' (or simply 'Prosper') network. It was set up in 1942 and headed by Francis Suttill, a London barrister with a British father and French mother. Suttill succeeded in establishing a large and highly effective group of anti-Nazi partisans, and throughout the early part of 1943 arms and agents flowed into France from Britain at a prodigious rate. As the group grew in influence, however, the risks of its discovery grew too. On 12 June 1943 an arms drop went badly wrong when a

Noor Inayat Khan, code-named 'Madeleine', captured by the Gestapo in 1943.

container exploded, and a local collaborator reported the event to the Gestapo. The area was flooded with over 500 Gestapo and SS men, who conducted house-to-house searches and arrested anyone they suspected of aiding the arms drop. Despite this, the British elected to parachute a further two SOE agents into the area just eight days later.

The SOE operative sent to meet the parachutists was Yvonne Rudelatt, the first female SOE agent parachuted into occupied France in the Second World War. An interior decorator from Kensington, London, Rudelatt was recruited while working as manageress of a London hotel at which many senior members of the SOE stayed. The SOE were keen to use women as agents as they were less likely to draw the suspicion of the Gestapo than men of military age out of uniform. Rudelatt quickly became vital to the SOE network in France and played a key role in several of the Resistance's most significant, and dangerous, operations. On 20 June 1943 she was tasked with picking up SOE agents Frank Pickersgill and John McAlister. The Germans were waiting for them. As the agents sped away from the drop-point, their car was showered with bullets and Rudelatt was struck twice. The bullet that lodged in her brain was too dangerous to remove, but her injuries were not life-threatening. She revealed nothing during her interrogation and was transported to Ravensbrück concentration camp. She died of typhus there shortly after the camp was liberated. At the time of her death she was still using her cover-name of Jacqueline Gautier and was buried in a mass-grave without being identified as an SOE agent.

A further wave of arrests and interrogations followed in

the wake of the capture of the SOE agents, however, and the information gleaned from them led the Gestapo to Francis Suttill. He was arrested, along with other key members of the Prosper network such as Andrée Borrel and Gilbert Norman. All were interrogated and Suttill was singled out for especially severe torture at the Gestapo headquarters at 84 Avenue Foch. After several days of brutal punishments he was transferred to Sachsenhausen concentration camp near Berlin where he was held in solitary confinement until his execution in March 1945.

Some writers have claimed that Suttill agreed to provide the Germans with information, while others maintain it was Gilbert Norman who cracked. Whatever the truth, hundreds of local agents were arrested over the next three months, of whom 80 were either executed immediately or died in concentration camps later. The Gestapo executed many captured agents as Allied forces moved through occupied Europe in 1945, and Norman and Borrel were among their victims. The Prosper network was shattered by the Gestapo's activities, with those agents who remained at large no longer sure which of their colleagues had been 'turned' by the threat of brutal torture. Communication back to Britain became incredibly difficult, and those receiving messages from the Prosper network were unsure if the agents transmitting were loyal or operating under instruction from Gestapo handlers.

Into this chaotic and highly dangerous situation was parachuted one of the SOE's most celebrated agents, Noor Inayat Khan, code-named 'Madeleine'. With most other radio operators captured or compromised, her work sending reliable messages back to Britain became vital. It allowed the British and French to begin to rebuild the Prosper network, which would prove crucial in the run-up to D-Day and the Allied advance through Normandy. Khan continued to broadcast despite the intense scrutiny of the Gestapo, who were well aware that a rogue wireless operator remained at large. She was eventually betrayed in October 1943, allegedly by a fellow female Resistance agent who was jealous of her relationship with a man in whom she shared an interest.

Khan was arrested by the Gestapo and a search of her home revealed a set of copies of her secret signals. This was entirely against her training and would prove disastrous in the coming months, as it allowed the Gestapo to send bogus messages to Britain and entrap further agents. They would face the same interrogation, torture, imprisonment and murder that was the hallmark of the Gestapo.

Khan was sent to Pforzheim prison in Germany in November 1943, where she was kept in chains in solitary confinement. Considered an especially unco-operative and dangerous prisoner, she gave no information and twice tried to escape from the Gestapo. On 12 September 1944 she was transferred to Dachau camp, where she was shot. Some reports suggest she was raped before her execution. Her remains were immediately taken to the camp crematorium. Britain awarded her the George Cross post-humously, and France honoured her with the Croix de Guerre.

In total there were 470 agents in the French section of the British SOE, 39 of them women. A total of 15 of these women were captured by the Gestapo, and 12 of those did not live to tell the tale. That means almost a third of female agents paid for their activities with their lives. By way of contrast, the figure for male agents was 18 per cent. This led some to suggest that female agents were deliberately 'sacrificed' by their handlers, in order to allow the Gestapo to get their hands on British wireless sets. The conspiracy suggests that the British used these sets to feed back erroneous messages about the location of the D-Day landings.

It is true that the campaign of deception launched by the Allies to convince the Nazis that they would land in Calais rather than Normandy was vast and full of intrigue. However, the overwhelming majority of the female agents undoubtedly contributed to the vital sabotage work that the Resistance did in order to ensure that the landings themselves succeeded. The high mortality rate they suffered as a consequence is almost certainly the result of the callousness of the Gestapo rather than an act of abandonment by the British Intelligence Services.

CHAPTER FIVE
PLOTS AND SUBPLOTS

By 1944, the Gestapo had over 30,000 employees. The Kripo had over 12,000 and the SD a little over 6,000. Despite the large number of staff, however, the police and intelligence services were permanently stretched. Men were desperately needed at the Eastern Front, which was by now absorbing vast numbers of soldiers as Hitler fought a bloody battle to the death with Stalin. In the west, Allied troops took Rome and then landed in Normandy to open a second front in the war. By August Paris was liberated and by October the Nazis had been driven out of Athens too. German forces launched a massive counter-attack in Belgium: it would later become known as the 'Battle of the Bulge'. Though it slowed the Allied advance, it failed to reverse it.

The war, then, was going badly for the Germans on all fronts. The Gestapo responded by now unleashing the same pitiless tactics it had used in the occupied territories upon the German Reich itself. Germans who had long since realized the futility of the war were cast as traitors to their country. Those identified as enemies of the state were subjected to a bloodthirsty frenzy of torture and execution. The Nazi regime, and the Gestapo in particular, was fighting for survival.

Stalag Luft III: Escape and Recapture

The site of the Luft III prison camp in Sagan, 160 km (100 miles) south-east of Berlin, was specially selected by the Luftwaffe for its most secure facility as it was considered near impossible to tunnel out of. The sandy soil in the area made any tunnels dug highly prone to collapse, and the sand was easy to detect, being bright yellow in marked contrast to the grey, dusty surface soil. The camp's remote location meant there was nowhere to tunnel to anyway. Or so it seemed.

The prison camp was guarded by Luftwaffe personnel, and was thus very different in character from those run by the Gestapo. While the guards were by no means the

Stalag Luft III, scene of 'The Great Escape', circa 1944.

cream of the German air force, they were fellow airmen who had a healthy respect for the Allied air force prisoners they watched over. Meagre food rations were sometimes an issue but other than that the prisoners were well treated. Despite this, however, many considered it their duty to try and escape and return to the frontline, and so an elaborate mass-escape plan was hatched. It consisted of the building of three separate tunnels, nicknamed 'Tom', 'Dick' and 'Harry'. As each of the prison barracks was elevated above ground as a security precaution, the tunnels were dug through stoves that were mounted on brick plinths.

It was a massive undertaking: each tunnel was dug at a depth of 9 m (30 ft) and when completed was 100 m (335 ft) long. The depth was necessary to avoid the microphones the Germans had buried in order to detect any digging noise. An extension to the camp covered Dick's planned exit point so it was abandoned and used to store the sand from the other tunnels and the equipment the escapers would need. Prior to this, prisoners nicknamed 'penguins' stuffed the sand down their trousers and distributed it around the prison yard as they walked on their breaks. The Germans eventually got wise to the practice and Tom was discovered, leaving only Harry as an escape option. The escape was originally planned for the summer, but the Gestapo visited the camp in early

1944 and advised increased security, so the date of the break-out was brought forward. The pilots would make their break for freedom as soon as Harry was finished.

That date was Friday, 24 March 1944. A moonless night increased the escapers' chances of evading detection. It had been hoped that hundreds would be able to make it out, but major problems with the plan soon emerged. The freezing March temperatures meant the tunnel's escape hatch had iced shut, and it took an hour and a half to force it open. Worse still, the tunnel was too short. The plan was for it to open in a nearby forest, but the actual exit was close to a sentry point. It left those emerging from the tunnel with a significant distance to cross in the open before reaching the forest. With snow on the ground, they would be highly visible.

Despite these problems – plus an air-raid alarm and a partial tunnel collapse – 76 airmen made it through the tunnel to freedom before the 77th was spotted, at 4.55 am on 25 March. An immediate inspection of the prison revealed that 4,000 bed boards had been broken up to provide supports for the tunnel. Countless articles of cutlery, bedding and furniture had also been utilized by the prisoners. Hundreds of metres of electric cabling, left unattended by German workers, had been stolen for use in the escape. The workers concerned were rounded up and shot by the Gestapo for failing to report the loss.

The incident was a grave embarrassment to the Nazi regime, and the Gestapo was determined to track down all of those who had escaped. According to the Geneva Convention, the maximum punishment allowable for escaped prisoners was 28 days in solitary confinement, but an incensed Hitler declared that all those who had escaped should be shot upon recapture. Eventually he was talked down by Göring and other senior Nazi figures, who pointed out that many German airmen were in the hands of the British and may be murdered in a tit-for-tat reprisal. Still, Hitler maintained that 50 of those who had escaped must be executed and immediately cremated as an example to the others. A national alert was ordered and Hitler's directive was teleprinted to Gestapo HQ by Himmler. A list of 50 names was then drawn up to satisfy their leader's order.

The Allied airmen were, quite literally, running for their lives. The thick snow in Sagan slowed their progress, and in the pitch-dark night many struggled to find the entrance to the local railway station, which was positioned in an unusual place, recessed under the train platforms. As a result, most of the escapers could not board night trains as planned. Many foreign workers used the trains, and the airmen had hoped to blend in with them. Instead they had to catch the first morning trains or slog their way out of Sagan on foot.

This combination of misfortunes for the Allied airmen made the Germans' task in capturing them considerably easier. In usual circumstances, escaped prisoners would be handed over to civilian police in order to be returned to their prison camp. The prisoners of Stalag Luft III, however, were all handed over directly to the Gestapo.

Of the 76 who emerged from the tunnel and fled into the night, just three managed to make it to safety and freedom. One by one the others were caught in the vast net that the Nazi regime had thrown across the area: 100,000 men were assigned to check the identities of every single person they encountered. Of those 73 recaptured, 17 were returned to Sagan, with another four being sent to Sachsenhausen concentration camp and two more to the infamous Colditz Castle.

The other 50 all suffered near-identical fates at the hands of the Gestapo. They were driven to remote locations, having been told they were being transferred to a distant camp. En route the Gestapo car would stop and the prisoners would be offered the opportunity to relieve themselves. As they turned their backs to do so they were shot in the back of the head. The Gestapo reports for each execution claimed the prisoners were shot while trying to escape. Half of those killed were British. Squadron Leader Roger Bushell – nicknamed 'Big X' and the man who originally conceived the 'Great

Escape' – was shot by Gestapo official Emil Schulz just outside Saarbrücken, Germany.

In due course the hunters would become the hunted: Allied forces placed the Gestapo executioners of the Stalag Luft III prisoners at the top of their wanted list after Germany lost the war. Foreign minister Anthony Eden had denounced the murders as a war crime and told the British Parliament:

His Majesty's Government must record their solemn protest against these cold-blooded acts of butchery.... They will never cease in their efforts to collect the evidence to identify all those responsible.... When the war is over, they will be brought to exemplary justice.

The Special Investigation Branch of the Royal Air Force Police hunted the perpetrators after the war with personal zeal – the only time a war crime was investigated by a single branch of any nation's military. They spent over three years chasing down leads and eventually identified 72 men who they believed were involved in the murders. A total of 21 Gestapo officers were duly executed after standing trial, with another 17 imprisoned. Of the rest, 11 committed suicide, six were killed during the war, five were arrested but charges were not brought, three were acquitted, one got a plea-bargain and one sought refuge in communist East Germany. Just seven remained untraced, though several of those were probably killed in the war.

The Ardeatine Massacre

On 3 September 1943, the Italians surrendered unconditionally to the invading Allied troops, and Hitler lost a key
European ally. The Germans rushed to reinforce their positions in Italy and quickly took control of Rome, imposing
Germany military law in the city. Fascist leader Benito
Mussolini was freed from prison and re-installed as a
puppet leader, to the consternation of many Italians who
had long since grown sick of war. The Italian Resistance
began to attack the occupying German and Fascist Italian
forces, and in retribution the Gestapo launched a series of
punitive raids against those thought to be responsible. In
January 1944, the Allies made a surprise landing at Anzio,
just 48 km (30 miles) from Rome, and an emboldened
Resistance redoubled its attacks. One of their more spec-
tacular successes was an operation launched on 23 March
1944 against a column of German soldiers marching
through the narrow street of Via Rasella in Rome.

A partisan disguised as a street cleaner pushed a rubbish
cart packed with TNT into the street, and 40 seconds later
it exploded, killing 28 soldiers and two civilians. Sixteen
partisans then traded fire with the Germans before melting
away into the back streets of Rome. The same evening,
senior German Secret Police officials decided that they
would retaliate by killing ten Italian civilians for every
German killed. As the death toll of the attack reached 33,

the Gestapo sifted through all available prisoners to decide which of them would be executed. When they discovered only four of those in their custody had been sentenced to death, they made up the numbers from others convicted of relatively minor crimes, and from Jews. The Gestapo, and their Nazi superiors, were concerned only with filling the huge quota that had been determined.

Doctors, lawyers, shopkeepers, artists and teenage boys were among those selected for murder. Some had simply had the misfortune to have been named as anti-Nazi by the Gestapo's vast network of informers. Perhaps the most famous victim of the massacre, however, was a key figure in the Italian Resistance and one of its most celebrated national heroes today. Colonel Giuseppe Montezemolo was the leader of the FRMC ('Clandestine Military Front of the Resistance') and had been in continual radio contact with the Italian government-in-exile until his arrest by the Gestapo on 25 January 1944. Like so many Gestapo victims before him, he had been brutally tortured in an attempt to glean further information on the Resistance's activities. Despite having his nails and teeth pulled out, he told them nothing. Another victim was General Simone Simoni, a 64-year-old war hero who endured being tortured with a blowtorch but refused to betray his Resistance comrades.

Due to a counting error, a total of 335 victims were

brought to the execution site, five more than the Gestapo's own barbaric mathematics had called for. The victims were taken in trucks to the Ardeatine caves on the rural outskirts of the city. With their hands tied behind their backs, they were led into the caves in groups of five and ordered to kneel down. The commanding officer had brought cases of brandy for his troops, to calm the nerves of men unused to cold-blooded murder. Each prisoner was killed with a single bullet to the back of the head. The cave was soon full of bodies, and those executed last had to kneel on the bodies of their fellow victims before being shot themselves. With 330 already dead, it was discovered that five extra prisoners had been brought to the scene. After a brief discussion, the men were shot anyway – to prevent any witnesses to the massacre reporting the location of the crime scene.

The bodies were placed in piles around a metre high and covered in rocks. German military engineers then set explosives to blast the cave rock and seal the entrance. Most of the relatives were told nothing about the fate of the prisoners. Those who were informed were given terse letters indicating only that their loved one was dead. The bodies lay undiscovered in the caves for over a year, until the Allies liberated Rome on 4 June 1944. Then a tip-off led investigators to the scene and the rubble was painstakingly removed in order to give the dead a proper burial.

Violette Szabo: Bravery and Defiance

Violette Szabo joined the British Special Operations Executive following the death of her highly decorated husband Étienne, who was killed in action during the Second Battle of El Alamein on 24 October 1942. Just a couple of months earlier, Violette had given birth to their first child, and she was inconsolable at the loss of the newborn's father. As she was French-born and fluent in both English and French, she was assigned to F-Section and trained as a field agent to work in Occupied France. She performed poorly in some aspects of training, and had to return home after spraining an ankle on her first parachute jump, but eventually passed through the SOE's 'finishing school' at Beaulieu in Hampshire. Like many female SOE agents, she enrolled with the First Aid Nursing Yeomanry (FANY) in order to disguise her connection with the Special Forces. Her cover story while in France was that she was a commercial secretary called Corinne Reine Leroy. She was parachuted into Cherbourg in Occupied France on 5 April 1944.

Standing just 1.6 m (5 ft 3 in) tall, she was nicknamed La Petite Anglaise, but it was her secondary nickname, 'Louise', that became her codename. Szabo and her SOE colleague Philippe Liewer (working under the cover name of 'Major Charles Staunton') were tasked with finding out what had happened to the 'Salesman'

Violette Szabo, captured by the Gestapo in 1944.

Resistance network, which had operated in Rouen and the northern coast of France. The network, co-founded by Liewer, was known to have been disrupted by wide-scale Gestapo arrests and the British were desperate to rebuild it before the critical Normandy landings in June. The Rouen area was considered too dangerous for Liewer to operate in as the Gestapo had his name and physical description, and so Szabo took a train to Paris and then on to Rouen alone. The mission was incredibly dangerous, and Szabo made her last will and testament before departing for France.

For the next few weeks she travelled extensively through the Rouen area, teeming as it was with German soldiers and Gestapo officers. Though she spoke perfect French, she did so with a thick Cockney accent and so had to be careful to keep her conversations with officials brief. Her physical beauty meant that she often drew the unwanted attention of strangers, and of German servicemen in particular.

Despite the danger and the difficulty, Szabo managed to reach all of the areas of interest to the British and ascertain which members of the Salesman network had fallen into the hands of the Gestapo. The information she provided on the state of the Resistance was of the utmost importance to the war effort, and in addition she managed to identify German munitions factories that would later become key targets for Allied bombers. Szabo discovered that the Salesman network had been decimated, with most of its key members having become victims of the Gestapo's 'Night and Fog' tactic and spirited away to Germany. She re-established a new network of Resistance agents and returned safely to Britain on 30 April 1944.

SOE was hugely impressed with Szabo's work, increased her salary and gave her a couple of weeks to rest and recuperate. With D-Day looming, however, she was soon pressed back into service. The network 'Salesman 2' was to be established in Haute Vienne and would concentrate on the strategic sabotage of railway lines and other infrastructure targets, to prevent the Germans being able to reinforce northern France once the Allied invasion began. Szabo was reunited with Liewer, who would head up the new network, with Violette acting as courier. They flew out to France on 7 June but were forced to turn back after the expected reception committee failed to show. On their return journey to England they flew over the vast invading fleet of Allied ships heading to the beaches of Normandy.

The next day the SOE agents successfully parachuted into France, which buzzed with the news of D-Day. The panicked Germans raced to shore up their defences and placed roadblocks on numerous roads into and out of the area. Szabo's mission was to contact the leader of another Resistance network ('Digger') in order to co-ordinate attacks on the German forces. She requested, and was given, a submachine gun in order to defend herself. The request was unusual as anyone carrying arms would undoubtedly be arrested if stopped by the Germans. Perhaps Szabo had already decided that events had moved beyond the stage of subterfuge and into the realms of open warfare.

The car she was travelling in with Jacques Dufour and Jean Bariaud, two other members of the Resistance, was stopped at a roadblock near the village of Salon-la-Tour. With Dufour and Szabo both heavily armed, allowing themselves to be stopped would result in their inevitable arrest. They elected to try and blast their way to freedom. Dufour brought the car to a halt and the three passengers leapt out, with Szabo and Dufour laying down withering machine-gun fire to cover their escape.

Bariaud, who was unarmed, managed to make a successful break for freedom in the ensuing mayhem. In time he would make contact with the rest of the Salesman network and warn them of the fate of his comrades. Szabo and Dufour broke away in the other direction, leaping a gate and running across a cornfield as German armoured cars swarmed to the scene of the gun battle. As the fugitives approached the relative safety of a forest, Szabo fell heavily and badly twisted her ankle. She refused Dufour's offer of help and insisted on covering his escape as best she could. For the next half an hour Szabo pinned down the massed German forces pursuing her, killing a German corporal and wounding several other soldiers.

Dufour used the time granted to him by Szabo's defensive fire well, and hid in the barn of a local Resistance sympathizer. One account suggests Szabo herself was taken to the same barn for interrogation after finally running out of ammunition. What is certain is that once disarmed she was taken into custody and gave her questioners the name of 'Vicky Taylor'. She was interrogated for four days at Gestapo headquarters in Limoges. When Dufour learned of her fate he organized a daring mission to rescue her. The plan was to attack the two guards who escorted her each day from Limoges prison to the Gestapo headquarters around half a mile away. Unfortunately, before the plan could be put into action, Szabo was moved to Fresnes prison in Paris, and from there to the infamous Gestapo HQ at 84 Avenue Foch.

The Gestapo by now knew the true identity of 'Vicky Taylor' and her links to the Special Operations Executive. She was interrogated relentlessly over the course of the next few days, and some assert that torture was also used on her. There is no conclusive evidence that she was physically harmed, but the pressure placed upon her to betray her comrades was doubtless intense. Despite this, Szabo gave the Gestapo no useful information. She carved her name in the wall of cell 45 to let others know she had been there, but aside from that we know nothing of her time at Avenue Foch. With the Allies pushing through Normandy towards Paris, it was decided that all prisoners of particular significance be evacuated back to Germany.

On 8 August Szabo was shackled at the ankles to another SOE agent, Denise Bloch, and placed on a train for the first part of the journey. Ironically the train narrowly avoided being hit by an Allied air raid en route. When her German guards leapt from the train in panic, Szabo took the opportunity to crawl along the floor of the train distributing water to her fellow prisoners, who were packed together in searing heat. Several later testified that her calmness, generosity and bravery were inspirational to them. With transportation badly disrupted due to the very sabotage she was in France to facilitate, her journey to Ravensbrück concentration camp took 18 days.

Most female SOE agents ended up at Ravensbrück, and Szabo suffered the same brutal conditions as the other prisoners. Ravensbrück's reputation was terrifying, with murder, torture and medical experimentation commonplace. Often made to work in freezing conditions, with only subsistence rations to draw energy from, the mortality rate among inmates was extremely high. Just three British SOE agents made it out of Ravensbrück alive, and Szabo was not among them.

Some time late in January or early February of 1945,

Szabo was summoned from her cell, along with her fellow agents Denise Bloch and Lilian Rolfe. By this time, Szabo was the only one of the three who could walk unaided. The three women were taken to a courtyard known to the prisoners as 'execution alley' and ordered to kneel. They held hands as each was shot in the back of the neck by a Gestapo officer. Immediately after their executions, they were stripped and cremated. Violette Szabo was 23 years old. When her death became known, she was awarded a posthumous George Cross by the British, and the Croix de Guerre by France.

July 20 and 'Operation Thunderstorm'

In part, the Gestapo grew from Hitler's fear that he would one day be betrayed by his own countrymen, and this concern was far from being a paranoid delusion. Ever since the Nazis' rise to power, certain parts of the German military machine had been secretly plotting to get rid of him. The resistance centred on the military intelligence organization the *Abwehr*. Many of the plotters were senior German armed-forces personnel who believed that the Fatherland would be destroyed if Hitler continued to pursue the war. They believed that if the fanatical leader was removed, Germany would be able to secure favourable peace terms with the Allies.

By the summer of 1944 it was clear to most Germans

Claus von Stauffenberg, the leader of 'Operation Valkyrie'.

that the war could no longer be won, and the only question remaining was whether the coming defeat would be total, or negotiated. Above all, those involved in the plot feared an invasion of Germany by the Soviet Union. A peace deal with the British and United States was considered infinitely preferable to that, and both allies had made clear that no deal would be done as long as Hitler was in power.

Though the plot is often termed 'Operation Valkyrie', that name in fact referred to the coup planned for the wake of Hitler's assassination. After Hitler's death, the plotters would occupy and take control of Germany's key ministries to prevent a breakdown in law and order or a counter-strike by the Nazis. For this plan to swing into action, of course, required the leader himself to be slain. This task fell to Lieutenant Colonel Claus Schenk Graf von Stauffenberg. He had been badly wounded in the North African campaign and was considered a war hero of impeccable standing. The Gestapo was incredibly suspicious of the more senior members of the *Abwehr*, and Stauffenberg was considered to stand a greater chance of getting close to Hitler. On 1 July 1944, Stauffenberg was appointed chief of staff to General Friedrich Fromm at the Reserve Army headquarters on Bendlerstrasse in central Berlin. This position enabled him to attend Hitler's military conferences. By the summer of 1944 the conspirators became aware that the Gestapo was closing in on them. It was now or never.

On 20 July 1944 the conspirators struck. At Hitler's *Wolfsschanze* ('Wolf's Lair') retreat in the Masurian woods of East Prussia, Stauffenberg brought a bomb to a military conference. The device was hidden in a briefcase, and primed by Stauffenberg in the bathroom of Field Marshal Wilhelm Keitel's office shortly before the conference began. Upon entering the conference room, Stauffenberg placed the briefcase under the table at which Hitler and 20 other senior Nazis were sitting. A few moments later, Stauffenberg excused himself from the meeting to make a telephone call. Ten minutes after Stauffenberg left the room, at around 12.45, the bomb detonated.

The conference room was devastated. However, the blast was deflected away from Hitler because the briefcase had been moved in Stauffenberg's absence. Placed behind a thick table leg, it killed four people in the room but left Hitler with only minor leg injuries and a perforated eardrum. Stauffenberg had originally intended to leave not one but two devices: had he done so, or had the first bomb not been moved, the plan would almost certainly have succeeded. Indeed, Stauffenberg, as he raced away from the complex towards Berlin, believed he had killed the Führer and that all was going to plan.

On one of the last planes to leave the area before aircraft were grounded, Stauffenberg had no way of contacting his fellow conspirators, nor did they have any way to contact him.

'Operation Valkyrie' now began to swing into action, but the conspirators were confused by conflicting messages about whether Hitler was dead or alive. The commander in chief of the Home Army responsible for implementing Valkyrie was 'Generaloberst' Friedrich Fromm, and he refused to do so without proof positive that Hitler was dead. Aware of the conspiracy, Fromm wanted to back whichever side was most likely to triumph, and he knew that if Hitler had indeed survived then any action against the Nazis at this point would be suicidal for him.

When Stauffenberg arrived, he exaggerated his story to claim that he had personally seen Hitler's body being taken from the conference room, and confessed to Fromm that he was the one who had placed the bomb. Instead of issuing the order to commence 'Operation Valkyrie', Fromm instead tried to arrest Stauffenberg, at which point Fromm himself was detained by two other conspirators who drew their pistols on him. Stauffenberg and fellow plotter General Friedrich Olbricht then tried to ring around to enact 'Operation Valkyrie' and spread the message that Hitler was indeed dead.

Attempts to wrest power from the Nazis floundered

once Himmler took personal control of the situation. He made it clear to all that Hitler remained in charge and that any disloyalty would be dealt with ruthlessly. By 7 pm Hitler had recovered enough to make phone calls to key personnel himself. The Bendlerblock building, home to the *Abwehr* and the meeting point for the conspirators, was surrounded. Stauffenberg was injured during the fighting that broke out; several other key plotters elected to commit suicide rather than face arrest.

Shortly after midnight, General Fromm was released from his armed detainment and he promptly ordered that Stauffenberg and the other plotters be arrested. Impromptu courts martial were held and Stauffenberg, Olbricht and two other officers were executed – probably to prevent them revealing the identities of others (including Fromm himself) involved in the plot. Many of the conspirators scrambled to distance themselves from those who had been directly involved in the day's events now that it was clear the plot had failed. It was in their interests to silence Stauffenberg before he could incriminate them.

They were right to be worried. A furious Hitler ordered Himmler to unleash the full power of the Gestapo in investigating the plot. He wanted every last link of the conspiracy tracked down and ruthlessly punished. The Gestapo operation that followed was one of the largest and most brutal that they ever embarked upon. In the coming days, weeks and months some 7,000 people were arrested, and the best estimate for the total executed is 4,980. Many had nothing whatsoever to do with the plot, but the Gestapo now had licence to settle any outstanding scores. On 23 August 1944, the investigation into the failed 20 July plot morphed into a wider purge of all those who might threaten the Reich's survival. 'Operation Thunderstorm' gave the Gestapo carte blanche to arrest and eliminate just about anyone they chose to. They leapt at the opportunity enthusiastically, in an environment of near-hysteria.

The first arrests, of those who organized the plot, resulted in show-trials and subsequent executions designed to be as demeaning and brutal as possible. Eight of those convicted (Robert Bernardis, Albrecht von Hagen, Paul von Hase, Erich Hoepner, Friedrich Karl Klausing, Helmuth Stieff, Erwin von Witzleben and Peter Graf Yorck von Wartenburg) were stripped naked and hanged with piano wire rather than rope. Their bodies were then hung on meathooks as the film cameras rolled. The footage was sent to Hitler, who replied with approval and urged the Gestapo on to root out each and every other conspirator.

Most of the thousands arrested were simply packed off to concentration camps and held without charge or trial. The bewildered 'enemies of the Reich' were often taken under 'Night and Fog' conditions, leaving their desperate families bereft of any information about their whereabouts. The Allies were by now close, pushing through Maastricht and Luxembourg, ever closer to the German border. For those opposed to the Nazi regime, liberation seemed tantalizingly near, yet many of those who most loathed Hitler were in the hands of his dreaded secret police.

The Gestapo's persecution of those associated with left-wing political views also intensified during the operation, as the unions had played a key role in the conspiracy. Their main representative, Wilhelm Leuschner, was interrogated and eventually executed for supporting the planned coup. His last word was 'Unity!' – but in the face of the Nazi terror police it was all too often 'every man for himself'. Known communists already being held in concentration camps were taken before firing squads and executed, in reprisal for the part their comrades had played in the conspiracy.

Anyone believed to be closely involved in the plot was treated with the utmost brutality by their Gestapo interrogators. Horrific torture caused many of them to crack, and gradually the names of all of the conspirators and sympathizers became known. Across Germany and those territories still occupied by German forces, wave after wave of arrests followed, producing further information, which led in turn to a further expansion of 'Operation Thunderstorm'.

In October 1944, Roland Freisler, the Gestapo's judge

of choice, was a busy man. Many of those arrested, interrogated and tortured by the Gestapo in the wake of the
plot were finally hauled before Freisler to receive their
inevitable death sentences. Among those condemned to
the firing squad were senior German officers Colonel Karl
Heinz Engelhorn, Major Adolf Friedrich Graf von Schack
and Lieutenant Colonel Wilhelm Kuebart. Even the notorious Freisler did not convict 100 per cent of those brought
before him, however. Some, such as Albrecht Fischer, who
offered to serve as commissioner for Stuttgart if the coup
succeeded, were found not guilty at trial. It made little
difference to the Gestapo: Fischer was simply re-arrested
and deported to Sachsenhausen concentration camp.
Though he survived and was liberated, most Gestapo
prisoners were shot as the Nazis retreated in the face of
the Allied troops in 1945.

Many other conspirators chose not to wait for the
Gestapo to break down their doors. Wessel Freiherr
Freytag von Loringhoven, the man who supplied
Stauffenberg with the explosives packed into the briefcase,
committed suicide in woods in East Prussia five days after
the failed plot, aware the Gestapo was closing in on him.

Even torture and death were not enough to satisfy
the Gestapo chief's thirst for revenge in the wake of the
20 July plot, though. On 4 August 1944, Heinrich
Himmler ordered that the remains of one of the plotters

executed on the night of the failed coup, Friedrich Olbricht, be exhumed. His body was then burnt and his ashes dispersed so that no physical trace of the traitor remained. The families of those involved in the assassination attempt were also targeted. Relatives of those executed after the 20 July plot were taken into custody and held in concentration camps. A total of 50 children related by blood to the conspirators were held in a 'children's home' in Bad Sachsa, where they remained until liberated by Allied forces in May 1945.

The Warsaw Uprising

As July 1944 drew to a close, Poland was in its fifth year of German occupation. The Red Army's spring offensive on the Eastern Front was driving Hitler's forces back to Warsaw's eastern suburbs, and the liberation of the country seemed close. In order to show that Poland was in solidarity with those fighting the Nazi tyranny, the Polish Underground Home Army decided to attack German forces in Warsaw. The offensive began on 1 August 1944, with some 40,000 Polish underground fighters, led by General 'Bor' Komorowski, taking part. The German garrison facing them numbered 15,000, but was better armed and better trained. The Poles believed they could drive the demoralized Germans from Warsaw. They were unaware that a decision had already been made to hold

A German staff car captured by the Polish Home Army during the Warsaw Uprising of 1944.

Warsaw at all costs, and that the city was critical in a German plan to counter-attack the Red Army.

German reinforcements poured into the city once the Polish insurgency began, and the defending garrison soon doubled in size to 30,000. Crucially, the Poles had only enough arms to support 2,500 of their fighters and enough ammunition to last for just one week of fighting. The Germans, on the other hand, were supported by tanks, planes and heavy artillery. The Soviet offensive halted 19 km (12 miles) from Praga, a suburb in east Warsaw, and as a consequence the Luftwaffe had the skies over the Polish capital to itself. The small and lightly armed

Polish Home Army would have to take on the might of the German military machine alone.

Over 180 German military installations were attacked by the insurgents, including the main military and police buildings, bridges, airports and train stations. In fierce and bloody fighting, the Germans managed to hold the most strategically important of their bases, but were forced to cede some significant strongholds in the city's west districts. By nightfall, the main post office and the high-rise Prudential building were in Polish hands, along with several key gas, electric and water works. Around 2,000 insurgents and 500 Germans lay dead. Crucially, the Germans had held out long enough for their reinforcements to arrive and for their forces to reorganize. The Poles no longer had the element of surprise on their side, and the battle for Warsaw would now enter a tragic new stage. The man in personal charge of the Warsaw operation from here on would be the head of the SS and Gestapo, Heinrich Himmler. Police and military units from all across the area were drafted in and given their orders: Warsaw was to be levelled, and the entire city's inhabitants slaughtered, as a warning to the rest of occupied Europe.

The German counter-offensive centred initially on the Wola and Ochota districts of Warsaw. German forces, primarily SS men and the Gestapo, rounded up 65,000 civilians in the captured districts. Under the supervision of the senior Gestapo officers, every man, woman and child was shot. Oskar Dirlewanger's homicidal SS *Sonderkommando* unit was one of those most heavily involved. The most notorious war crimes perpetrated during this stage of the campaign occurred at the district hospitals, where an estimated 1,360 patients and staff were murdered. The Radium Institute Hospital was attacked at just after ten o'clock on the morning of 5 August. The female staff were dragged into the hospital gardens and raped, while the male staff and all patients capable of walking were kept outside at gunpoint for four days in freezing conditions. They were then transported to concentration camps in Germany. The patients unable to move were shot in their beds, and the mattresses set on fire beneath them. Many not killed by the gunfire were burnt alive. The Germans then burnt the entire hospital to the ground, leaving the 70 or so patients trapped on the upper floors to die amidst the flames. Others captured were lined up in threes, and a Gestapo officer shot them, one by one, in the back of the head.

Drunken German troops also burst into the Wola hospital and machine gunned all those within sight. The remaining patients and staff were marched to a nearby house and relieved of any of their valuables. Around 500 were shot in batches of 12 or so. The dead included patients, staff, priests and nuns. Grenades were thrown into the pile of bodies and the house then burnt to the ground. The following day, tanks levelled the site. Himmler's orders to murder everyone in Warsaw and destroy every building were methodically carried out as the German troops moved remorselessly through the city. Some unfortunate civilians were hung from lampposts after having been beaten, whipped and raped. Photographs were taken of the events so that the Nazi elite would be satisfied at the level of murder and destruction.

One woman who miraculously survived the slaughter despite being shot in the head later described how the Germans sang and drank amidst the piles of bodies. They kicked the lifeless corpses to check for any signs of life, before taking any valuables that had hitherto been missed. Later, in order to save ammunition for the battle against the Polish Home Army, the Germans developed a new tactic for their mass murders: burning the residents of Warsaw alive. Houses and large buildings were surrounded from all sides, and then gasoline and grenades were thrown into them. Those who rushed out to flee the flames were mown down with machine guns. Most of those not killed in the initial fireball died of smoke inhalation, or later in hospital from their severe burns.

There were widespread reports of the Germans using large groups of civilians as 'human shields'. Mostly women, children and the elderly, they were forced to stand or kneel across Warsaw's streets so that the German troops could fire on the insurgents from behind them. The Germans had learned to their cost on the Eastern Front just how bloody street-to-street fighting could be and were determined to minimize their losses. Their brutal tactics made the job of the Polish Home Army far more difficult, yet many later testified to the almost miraculous accuracy of the Polish snipers. German troops were bewildered by the fact that their own side appeared to be struck with bullets from all directions, while their Polish hostages remained unharmed.

The insurgents battled on, despite the odds and their dwindling ammunition supplies. Communication between the various pockets of Resistance was maintained through the city's network of sewers. The British made over 200 sorties to air-drop vital supplies to the Resistance, but Prime Minister Winston Churchill's pleas to Franklin Roosevelt and Stalin for co-ordinated Allied assistance fell on deaf ears. Until the middle of September, all captured Polish Resistance fighters were executed on the spot rather than treated as prisoners of war. Stukas dive-bombed all areas under Polish control, including clearly marked hospitals.

Despite the Germans' determination to crush Polish morale through their brutality, the Poles managed to capture the ruins of the Warsaw ghetto and free 350 Jews from the Gesiówka concentration camp. Many of the city's residents were evacuated through the sewer system, which the Home Army used themselves in order to gradually fall back in the face of the German onslaught. The Red Army reached the east bank of the Vistula river in mid-September, but the retreating German army blew up all the bridges to prevent further progress. The Soviets provided only sporadic artillery and air support to the Resistance. On 18 September Stalin rescinded the ban on the Western Allies landing on Soviet territory, and the United States Air Force dropped supplies to the Resistance for the first time. But it was too little too late: by now the Polish forces were too thin and too widely dispersed to do anything but withdraw.

Capitulation finally came on 2 October, with the Germans agreeing to treat the combatants according to the Geneva Convention in return for their surrender. Around 15,000 of them were disarmed and sent to prisoner-of-war camps in Germany. The entire civilian population of Warsaw was expelled from the city and sent to a transit camp. Up to half a million people were sent from the transit point to labour camps, concentration camps and assorted other holding facilities throughout Germany. Then German demolition squads moved in. Flamethrowers were used to burn all the major buildings left standing, and the rest of the city was dynamited into rubble. Around 85 per cent of the buildings in Warsaw were destroyed.

The casualty figures on both sides can only be estimated, but it is widely believed that around 20,000 combatants died on each side. Due to the brutality of the Gestapo and SS forces, the Polish civilian casualties were far higher – some put the figure as high as 200,000.

The Betrayal of Anne Frank

On 4 August 1944, four Gestapo officers raided a canal warehouse at 263 Prinsengracht, Amsterdam. Inside they found eight Jewish people hiding in an annexe: Otto Frank, his wife and two children; the three members of the van Pels family; and a dentist by the name of Fritz Pfeffer. The Gestapo took them first to Westerbork camp and then on to the notorious concentration camp at Auschwitz. Of the eight people arrested, only Otto Frank survived the war. His daughter, Anne Frank, would later become one of the most widely known victims of the Gestapo, thanks to the diary she kept during her time in hiding.

It is believed the famous Anne Frank diary was dumped from Otto's briefcase when a Gestapo officer emptied it in order to fill it with the fugitives' valuables. It was later picked up by Miep Gies, one of the Dutch citizens who helped the Frank family hide, and she returned it to Otto Frank after the end of the war.

The diary chronicles Anne's life from her 13th birthday in 1942 until the moment of her capture. Though extraordinarily powerful thanks to Anne's personal style, the story of the Frank family is typical of thousands of other Jewish families during the Second World War. Born in Germany, Anne Frank moved with her family to the Netherlands when the Nazis came to power in 1933. They then became trapped when the Nazis occupied the country in 1940. When the persecution of the Jewish population by the Gestapo intensified, the family went into hiding. From 1942 until their arrest in 1944, they hid in an annexe hidden behind a bookcase in the building where Otto Frank worked.

Who, exactly, betrayed the family is a mystery. In truth, there is no shortage of candidates. The Gestapo relied heavily on its network of informants in all the territories it policed. Many collaborated because they were double agents, 'turned' by the heavy-handed interrogation techniques of the secret police. Others gave the Gestapo information in return for favourable treatment or black-market goods. After their arrest, the Franks were taken to the RSHA headquarters and interrogated. Having been caught hiding, they were considered criminals and shipped to Auschwitz, where Otto was separated from the rest of the family. It was here that

Anne became aware of the full horror of the gas chambers, though she herself was not selected for immediate execution. Instead, she and her sister Margot were transferred to the concentration camp at Belsen, leaving behind their mother, who was by that time too ill to be moved. Edith Frank died shortly afterwards.

Little is known of Anne and Margot's time in the concentration camps, but they both died before the Allies liberated the camps in 1945. It is most likely that Anne died in February 1945, of typhus, starvation or a combination of both. When last seen she was bald, emaciated and demoralized by the death of her mother – she believed her father was also dead, though in fact he survived his period in Auschwitz. Anne Frank was one of an estimated 107,000 Jews deported from the Netherlands during the Nazi occupation. Tragically, she was also one of the estimated 102,000 who perished in the German concentration camps. Like most of these, she was unceremoniously buried in a mass grave.

In 1963, Karl Silberbauer was identified as the commander of the Gestapo raid that arrested Anne Frank and her family. He was not prosecuted for his role in the death of the war's most famous diarist, however. Anne Frank's father Otto stated that Silberbauer had 'only done his duty and behaved correctly' during the arrest.

CHAPTER SIX
BREAKING THE CHAIN

The chain of command from the RSHA down to the provincial Gestapo offices rapidly fell apart as the Allies overran occupied territories and finally Germany itself. Relentless Allied bombing shattered the Nazi command and control structure. Prior to the war, the regional offices had always had far greater autonomy, but in the war years they had come to rely on orders from above. When that culture changed, the Gestapo struggled to adapt. Confusion rapidly turned to panic in the areas farthest from Berlin, and in regions where adherence to the Nazi philosophy was less fanatical than in the capital. Information often arrived too late to be of use to officers, or could not be acted upon even if it did arrive in time due to increasing shortages of staff. The ruthless efficiency that had characterized the Gestapo ebbed away, and with it its air of invincibility.

When Germany surrendered, the key figures of the reviled Gestapo were hunted down remorselessly by the Allies, and many of their stories are included here. The 'rank and file' members of the organization were rarely punished harshly, however. Thousands of former SS and Gestapo men found employment in the intelligence services and the civil services of both West and East Germany. A law passed in 1948 in West Germany granted amnesty for all crimes committed before 15 September 1949 for which the punishment was less than six months. As many as 700,000 convicts and suspects benefited as a result.

The Demise of Roland Freisler

By 1945, the Allies had forced the Luftwaffe onto the back foot and begun to take control of the skies over Western Europe: even the German capital was no longer safe from attack. One particular raid on 3 February was to have a major impact on the Gestapo, killing one of its best-known and most flamboyant associates, Judge Roland Freisler.

It was 'Raving Roland' Freisler who routinely handed down death sentences to the defendants brought before him by the Gestapo, often without any evidence of guilt being offered. A fanatical Nazi, Freisler was known for his angry outbursts at those in the dock, and for ruthlessly punishing anyone who dared to show disloyalty to Hitler. In one especially memorable instance, a young woman named Marianne Elise Kürchner was arrested by the Gestapo for making a joke about the Führer. She reportedly said, 'Hitler and Göring are standing atop the Berlin radio tower. Hitler says he wants to do something to put a smile on Berliners' faces. So Göring says, "Why don't you jump?".'

Freisler's judgement upon her? 'Her honour has been

permanently destroyed,' he said in his adjudication, 'and therefore she shall be punished with death.' As far as Freisler was concerned, the war was no laughing matter.

It is perhaps fitting that the Gestapo's chief judge lost his life while in the process of sitting in judgement on one of those arrested in the wake of the 20 July plot to assassinate Hitler. The wave of arrests that followed the attempted coup was one of the most notorious Gestapo operations. One of those interrogated and tortured was Fabian von Schlabrendorff, who had been a member of the German Resistance for several years and had unsuccessfully tried to assassinate Hitler in March 1943. A primed bomb he passed to one of Hitler's associates was supposed to blow his plane out of the sky, but it was left in the drawer of his desk, where in any case it failed to detonate.

Schlabrendorff was facing a certain death sentence from Freisler when an Allied air raid caused the trial to be halted. The unsentenced defendant was hurried away to a cell and spent the rest of the war being shuffled between detention camps, before being liberated by the Allies. Judge Freisler, however, deemed that he had time enough to pick up his paperwork before evacuating the court building after the suspension of Schlabrendorff's trial. It was a fatal mistake.

A direct hit on the building caused a roof beam to fall

on Freisler, who subsequently died of his injuries. The bombing raid was led by US Air Force pilot Robert Rosenthal, a Jew who later worked as an assistant to a prosecutor at the Nuremberg trials. A hospital worker who received Freisler's body was reported to have remarked, 'It is God's verdict.' It was certainly a verdict that Freisler himself had handed down to others on thousands of occasions during the war.

'Operation Carthage'

The Danish Resistance movement (*Modstandsbevægelsen*) had long requested that the Allies target the Gestapo headquarters in the 'Shell House' (*Shellhus*) building in Copenhagen. By March 1945 the British had both the means and the will to carry out such a raid, having perfected the art of high-speed, low-level bombing runs with Mosquito aircraft. Even so, it was an incredibly audacious and high-risk attack, involving a flight in broad daylight right into the heart of a major city that was heavily defended with anti-aircraft guns.

The Gestapo, however, was holding dozens of high-level Danish Resistance fighters and the building was packed with dossiers that could lead to the execution of hundreds more. The Shell House was notorious as a centre of torture and depravity, and as a symbol of Nazi oppression in Denmark. The plan was to badly

The Shellhus, Copenhagen headquarters of the Gestapo in Nazi-occupied Denmark, on fire in the aftermath of the 'Operation Carthage' bombing raid by the RAF, 21 March 1945.

disrupt the Gestapo's operation in the country while freeing the Resistance prisoners. The Gestapo held the majority of the prisoners on the top floor of the building, as 'human shields' against bombers, so the RAF decided to precision-bomb only the lower floors.

Three waves of six RAF Mosquitoes took part in the raid, supported by 30 American-supplied Mustang fighters. The latter's role was not only to provide cover against enemy aircraft but also to attack and draw fire from the anti-aircraft guns positioned all across the city. Given the Shell House's location in the centre of a densely populated area, the bombers would have to fly as low as possible. Indeed, as testament to this, one of the Mosquitoes crashed after its wing clipped a 30 m (100 ft)-high lamppost. Tragically, it spun out of control into the nearby Jeanne d'Arc School and burst into flames. Some of the following waves of bombers, seeing the flames, mistook the burning school for their target and dropped their bombs there. As a result, 86 schoolchildren and 18 adults (most of whom were nuns) were killed.

Many of the bombers, however, did score direct hits on the Gestapo HQ, and caused massive damage to the building. As it burnt, 18 Resistance prisoners took the opportunity to escape. A total of 55 Germans were killed, along with 47 Danish Gestapo employees and eight prisoners. One of the prisoners killed was Morgens Prior, who was being beaten by the Gestapo when the raid interrupted the torture. The badly wounded Prior died after jumping from the window of his fourth-floor interrogation room. The RAF lost four Mosquitoes and two Mustangs in the raid, which left nine airmen dead.

The role of the Danish Resistance has long been a source of historical debate, with many suggesting that Denmark did little to resist the Nazi occupation, while others point to the high quality of the information the Danes supplied to Britain. The most celebrated Danish Resistance fighter, Bent Faurschou Hviid (nicknamed 'Flammen' or 'the Flame' due to his bright red hair), was certainly a thorn in the side of the Gestapo. Widely believed to have personally executed 22 Nazi collaborators and double agents, Flammen was the most wanted man in Denmark until his death in October 1944. The bounty on his head led to his betrayal, and though he fled across a roof, he soon realized he was surrounded. Faurschou Hviid swallowed cyanide rather than face the Gestapo torture chambers. His lifeless body was dragged off the roof and down the stairs by its feet, with the arresting officers cheering each time his head struck a stair.

The remaining Danish Resistance fighters later succeeded in disrupting the Danish railway network in the days following D-Day, preventing German troops stationed in the country from reinforcing the Nazi defences in Western Europe.

The Case of Wernher Von Braun

The Gestapo's arrest of Germany's chief rocket scientist, Wernher von Braun, in March 1945, would arguably change the entire world. Throughout the war, von Braun was in charge of developing advanced rocket-based weapons that Hitler hoped would give the Reich a decisive military edge. Von Braun's brilliance resulted in the V-2 rocket, the world's first long-range guided ballistic missile. As the tide of war turned, the V-2 rockets were increasingly viewed as the wonder-weapon that might force the Allies to make peace with Germany rather than force the country to unconditionally surrender. More than 3,000 of the rockets were launched between September 1944 and the spring of 1945, initially targeted at London but later also at Antwerp and Liège. The number of people killed by the weapons is estimated at between 5,000 and 9,000.

Though the V-2 was effective as a terror weapon, it was too inaccurate to bring the kind of devastation of which Hitler dreamed. In addition, the production of the V-2 was horribly expensive, in terms of both treasure and blood. The Reich spent the equivalent of around £3 billion ($4.6 billion) in today's terms, and in excess of 10,000 forced labourers were killed while working on the project, from exhaustion, sickness, malnutrition and mistreatment.

Senior members of the Gestapo believed that von Braun was more interested in the potential for rockets to travel into space than he was in rocket-powered weaponry. Himmler had a burning personal desire to get his hands on the technology and pushed to be allowed to take control of the entire operation. When this route brought him no joy he planted the suggestion that von Braun was deliberately dragging his feet on the rocket project. A rumour was also spread that von Braun was in fact a British spy about to betray the secret technology to the British.

Hitler was unnerved enough to allow Himmler to arrest von Braun and interrogate him. The entire team behind the V-2 was raided at 2 am and hauled into Gestapo headquarters while their homes and workplaces were searched. Von Braun remained in 'protective custody' for over two weeks, but no evidence of the supposed plan to flee to England was discovered by the Gestapo investigation. Eventually Hitler ordered his release, and von Braun returned to work. He was still involved in the V-2 project when he surrendered to Allied forces in 1945, along with his brother Magnus and the rest of his team.

Because of Himmler's accusations and von Braun's imprisonment by the Gestapo, the German scientist was treated favourably by the United States army. He and his team were flown to America, where he eventually became technical director of the US army Ordnance

Guided Missile Project in Alabama. Von Braun designed the Saturn V booster that in 1969 sent Apollo 11 to the moon. By then he was a US citizen, and his past close association with the Nazi regime was a distant memory. His rehabilitation after the war was undoubtedly helped by Himmler, whose paranoid accusations provided von Braun with an anti-Nazi cover story that he never really had. As a result, the Gestapo inadvertently helped the United States win the space race, 25 years after they raided their chief rocket scientist's home.

Justice for Hermann Fegelein

Hermann Fegelein was a career opportunist who took advantage of his close links to those in power in order to rise up through the ranks of the Nazi military machine. He was the brother-in-law of Hitler's partner (and future wife) Eva Braun, and thus part of Hitler's inner circle. In addition, he cultivated a close friendship with Heinrich Himmler, who ensured that he received the positions he most coveted in the Reich.

When Fegelein faced court-martial charges in 1940 after stealing food and luxury goods, Himmler stepped in to ensure all charges against his friend were dropped. Gestapo head Reinhard Heydrich tried on several occasions to have Fegelein brought to justice for a variety of crimes, including 'murder motivated by greed'. That

Hermann Fegelein, who benefited from his acquaintance with Hitler through Eva Braun, Hitler's partner and subsequently his wife.

charge related to Fegelein ordering the execution of several prisoners held in a Gestapo prison so that he could take possession of their valuables. However, Fegelein was too well connected for any of the charges to stick.

Fegelein's SS *Totenkopf Reiterstandarte* ('Death's-Head Horse Regiment') worked closely with the German state police forces, including the Gestapo. While his unit was deployed in Poland it took part in the Kampinos Forest massacre that saw 1,700 Polish intellectuals shot dead. When the unit later moved to the Eastern Front, it assisted the Gestapo in rounding up partisans, Jews and suspected communists and executed them without trial. In offensive action Fegelein was daring to the point of recklessness, and was wounded by a Red Army sniper before being more severely wounded on 30 September 1943 during defensive actions against the Soviets.

Following his convalescence, Fegelein was moved from frontline duties and Himmler made him liaison officer and chief representative of the SS at Hitler's headquarters. He was one of those seated round Hitler's table during the failed assassination attempt on 20 July 1944. Fegelein, like Hitler himself, escaped with only minor wounds. For the rest of his life he kept photographs of those rounded up by the Gestapo and hanged in the wake of the failed coup. As the Allied and Soviet forces encircled Berlin in April 1945, Fegelein was at Hitler's side in the Führerbunker, but ever the opportunist, he saw the writing on the wall and was determined not to go down with the sinking ship.

On 27 April 1945, it was noticed that Fegelein was not in the Führerbunker as usual. One of Hitler's bodyguards, Peter Högl, was sent out to see what had happened to him. Upon arriving at Fegelein's Berlin apartment, Högl found him dressed in civilian clothes. Fegelein had been drinking heavily and was seemingly planning to flee to Switzerland or Sweden. His packed bags were found to contain large amounts of cash and jewellery – some of which belonged to his wife. Even worse, a briefcase in Fegelein's possession revealed evidence of Himmler's attempts to negotiate peace with the Western Allies.

Himmler's relationship with Hitler had been strained ever since the Führer had placed the Gestapo chief in charge of halting the Red Army's advance into Pomerania, a region today split between Poland and Germany. Himmler proved to be a disastrous military commander and was easily defeated by his opposing number, Marshal Georgy Zhukov. As the German forces desperately tried to flee across the Baltic Sea, Himmler began to send increasingly incoherent reports back to Hitler. He eventually suffered a nervous breakdown and fled to a sanatorium, further eroding Hitler's confidence in him.

The two men met for the last time on Hitler's birthday, 20 April 1945, when Himmler learned that Hitler intended to stay in Berlin and fight to the death rather than attempt to escape. Himmler swore loyalty to his leader but had no intention of joining his suicide pact. Instead he began secret negotiations with Count Folke Bernadotte, the head of the Swedish Red Cross, about a possible German surrender. Without Hitler's knowledge, Himmler agreed to the repatriation of thousands of concentration camp prisoners to the safety of neutral Sweden. Then, claiming to be the provisional leader of Germany, Himmler signed a surrender document, seeking to ensure that it was the Allies rather than the Soviets who entered Germany.

Himmler's negotiations would not be made public until a BBC news item the day after Fegelein's arrest. Once Himmler's treachery was confirmed, his representative, Fegelein, was doomed. Hitler was enraged at what he saw as disloyalty all around him, and ordered Himmler to be stripped of all military ranks and arrested. Fegelein, who for so long had worked hand in hand with the Gestapo, was now to face one of its most feared interrogators, Heinrich Müller.

According to most accounts, a tearful and intoxicated Fegelein claimed merely to be Himmler's messenger and not to be directly involved in his peace plans. At least one report suggests that Hitler's partner, Eva Braun, pleaded on behalf of her brother-in-law, and as a result Hitler reversed a decision to sentence Fegelein to death. This account states that Hitler wanted Fegelein demoted and ordered him to prove his loyalty by fighting the Soviet invasion of Berlin. When others pointed out that Fegelein would simply desert and flee, Hitler changed his mind again.

Fegelein was brought out of his makeshift cell at the Führerbunker to face a hastily arranged court martial. Waffen-SS General Wilhelm Mohnke presided over the trial and, sympathetic to Fegelein's plight, concluded that the petrified defendant was in no fit state to stand trial. He ordered the proceedings to be closed and handed Fegelein over to General Rattenhuber and his security squad, with instructions that he be detained.

Exactly what happened thereafter is the subject of much debate. All accounts agree that at some point on 28 April Fegelein was taken into the garden of the Reich Chancellery and shot. Some reports suggest that this was done on Hitler's orders, others that a further court martial found him guilty of treason and sentenced him to death. The last survivor from the Führerbunker, body-guard Rochus Misch, later claimed to know the identity of Fegelein's executioner, but refused to reveal his name.

He stated that Fegelein was 'shot like a dog' and killed by a single bullet to the back of the head.

By the time Fegelein met his bloody end, the Soviets had advanced to Potsdamerplatz, just 300 m (330 yd) from the Reich Chancellery. News of this, combined with Himmler and Fegelein's disloyalty, prompted Hitler to write his last will and testament. Two days later, he shot himself in the head. The Germans surrendered unconditionally to the Allies on 7 May. After six catastrophic years, the war in Europe was finally over.

CHAPTER SEVEN
LAST DAYS OF THE GESTAPO

With the collapse of the German army on both the Eastern and Western Fronts came the collapse of the Gestapo from within. Gradually the chain of command, which throughout the war had been so rigid and dependable, dissolved. The Reich Security Main Office (RSHA) was obliged to pass responsibility for key decisions further and further down the Gestapo ranks. From February 1945 onwards, newly appointed 'Commanders of Security Police' (*Kommandeure der Sicherheitspolizei*) had the power to condemn almost anyone to death without trial. Middle-ranking officers were suddenly faced with momentous decisions they had no experience of dealing with. They reacted, in general, by copying the actions of their superiors – and often even outdoing them in terms of inhumanity. The result was a wave of mass executions as the Gestapo units retreated back towards Berlin.

In the Ruhr region of north-west Germany, a particular problem for the Gestapo was foreign workers. Most of these were forced into work after having been captured in the occupied territories of the east. Many were from the Soviet Union, and as such were associated with the very forces now threatening the future of the Reich on its eastern border. As the Western Allies and Red Army remorselessly rolled towards the German capital, revenge was in the air. Workers from the east bore the brunt of the Gestapo's frustrations, as they were considered to be of an inferior bloodline, and the Soviet armed forces had a not-undeserved reputation for brutality against captured Germans. Hundreds of such foreign workers were rounded up by the Gestapo and executed with a bullet to the back of the neck.

The most commonly cited reason for the executions related to maintaining public order. As the iron grip of the Gestapo began to weaken, groups of workers banded together to form armed gangs. They looted shops and factories and were frequently involved in shoot-outs with the security forces. With food and other supplies running critically short, there was little choice for some but to steal what they could. Many entirely innocent workers were thus tarred with the same brush and accused of looting or belonging to the burgeoning Resistance movement. The standard Gestapo response of an excessive show of force was deployed to try to prevent a slide into chaos.

The Gestapo's prisons were overflowing with prisoners even before the panic induced by the Allied armies' approach. Moving large numbers of inmates farther east, away from the frontline, was a logistical nightmare. Instead, large numbers were simply executed. Between the end of March and mid-April, almost all of the large cities in the Ruhr region saw mass executions. The best-documented examples serve here merely as an illustration of the widespread carnage wrought by the Gestapo in its final days.

In early February, 24 members of a group known as the 'Kovalenko gang' were shot in Duisburg, although many other prisoners there accused of minor offences were released. The chief of police decided who would live and who would die. Those in the latter category included 29 prisoners (including several women) who had allegedly provided shelter for the gang. They were marched to a nearby bomb crater and mown down by Gestapo officers with machine pistols. Though the Ruhr region was not short of bomb craters by this point in the war, soon the Gestapo would run out of these for use as execution sites. A further 38 eastern workers and German inmates were shot in Duisburg alone before the Gestapo fled the area.

In Essen, a 'special police court' was convened by the local Gestapo chiefs and 35 prisoners were condemned to death. They were taken to the 'Monday hole' near Gruga Park the next day and executed. The head of the Gestapo in Essen, Peter Nohles, ensured that those who pulled the triggers were police officers who had never previously been involved in executions. He wanted all of his underlings to be complicit in the bloody crimes in order to establish their loyalty. Doubtless he feared that anyone not directly involved might testify against him in future. Nohles was one of the main architects of the transport of Jews out of Essen and must have known that he would soon be brought to account for his actions. In the end he could not evade justice and elected to die by his own hand in 1947.

Similar scenes took place in other cities in the area, with the wave of executions reaching its climax in Dortmund, where the Gestapo's main office was located. In its prisons the Gestapo held hundreds of prisoners, including members of the local Resistance movement and those accused of spying. The overwhelming majority, however, were prisoners of war and labourers, mostly from Russia. Though no one knows exactly how many were executed in Dortmund in the final weeks of the war, the Gestapo's own meticulous records indicate that at least 230 were shot in the back of the neck and buried in bomb craters. The last executions took place in open fields where they could easily be witnessed, as the more discreetly located bomb craters were by this time already full of bodies. Many of the executed workers were females. The last three were shot close to the railway station on 8 or 9 April, just before the Gestapo officers boarded trains out of

Dortmund, as the first Allied troops entered the fringes of the city.

The chosen rendezvous point for the retreating Gestapo in the Ruhr region was the local high school at the garrison town of Hemer. A vast prisoner-of-war camp there held more than 200,000 inmates throughout the six years of the war, more than 24,000 of whom, as a result of the appalling conditions, ended up being buried close by. The Gestapo had always been a paranoid organization, but now that the writing was on the wall for the Nazi Reich, the secret police's mistrust spread to the German population in general, and even to fellow Gestapo officers. Gestapo men began to melt away and disguise themselves as civilians, or else to accuse one another of disloyalty or cowardice.

In the commandeered school house at Hemer, the mistrust reached almost farcical proportions. The staff of the various Gestapo offices in the Ruhr essentially found themselves guarding not prisoners but one another. Each office suspected that their colleagues in other offices were planning to run off rather than await instructions from their superiors. It became impossible to police the streets because all available officers were needed to watch one another for signs of desertion.

The thousands of executions carried out in the last weeks of the war cannot be fully explained in purely rational terms. There is no doubt that many of the killings were simply down to the cold psychopathic logistics of the organization: prisoners could not be easily evacuated, and so they were murdered. However, they could just as easily have been released en masse to be dealt with by the rapidly approaching liberation armies. Some may have been killed to prevent them testifying against members of the Gestapo, but again the rationale is flawed, as the Gestapo was well aware that no matter how many were killed there would still be plenty of witnesses to the organization's crimes left alive. It is difficult not to conclude that spite and vengeance motivated much of the slaughter. Senior Gestapo officers knew that they had no future after the war in a defeated Germany, and simply elected to take as many people as possible down with them.

The situation changed with Hitler's suicide and the subsequent surrender of Germany. Now, it was every man for himself. The hunters had become the hunted.

In Pursuit of the Gestapo

The Western Allies had specialist teams who sifted through prisoners of war looking for key members of the Gestapo. Those successfully captured would later stand trial at Nuremberg. The Soviets had a reputation for being more severe, and many Gestapo agents who fell into their hands were never heard of again. The majority were probably executed on the spot, though hundreds more were sent to Stalin's brutal Gulag camps. Those who had collaborated with the Gestapo often suffered summary justice at the hands of their fellow citizens or members of the local Resistance. It was not uncommon throughout occupied Europe for informants and collaborators to be paraded through the streets with signs hung around their necks before being hanged or shot.

In such an environment, many Gestapo men elected to seek out Allied forces and surrender willingly to them. The most senior figure to do so was Herman Göring, the man who for much of the war was second-in-command to Hitler and his chosen heir. He was taken into custody near Radstadt on 6 May after surrendering to the 36th Infantry Division of the US Army. Had Göring not done so, he may well have been executed by his own side: Hitler's private secretary, Martin Bormann, had sentenced him to death for treason. Göring had been stripped of all ranks and condemned as a traitor after attempting to assume control of the Reich shortly before Hitler's suicide.

Once in custody, Göring was flown to a prisoner-of-war camp in Luxembourg to be interrogated and weaned off the 320 mg of dihydrocodeine (a morphine derivative) he took daily. He would be the most high-profile official to stand trial at Nuremberg (though only the second-highest-ranking, after former Admiral Karl Dönitz was made Reich President in the wake of Hitler's suicide).

Heinrich Himmler was the next most senior figure on the Allies' wanted list, and on 22 May 1945 he was arrested along with two others at a British checkpoint at the Bremervorde Bridge. This was the only bridge left standing between Bremen and Hamburg, and Himmler intended to use it in order to reach the Bavarian mountains and escape. Himmler was using the name Heinrich Hitzinger, but drew attention to himself because of his curious appearance: he had a patch over one eye and several days of beard growth, and was dressed in an 'odd collection of civilian garments with a blue raincoat on top'. Under interrogation, the three prisoners contradicted one another's stories, and in due course Himmler removed his eye patch and admitted his true identity.

The British were well aware that many senior Nazis carried cyanide capsules to swallow as a last resort. Himmler was searched and two cyanide capsules were found on him and removed. He was then transferred to the British headquarters where a military doctor began a more thorough examination of the prisoner. It was at this point that Himmler bit down on a cyanide capsule that was embedded in one of his teeth. Despite frantic efforts to save him, he died 12 minutes later. Himmler's body was buried in secret by the British to prevent it ever becoming a Nazi shrine. To this day, nobody knows the location of his final resting place.

The Allies were deeply concerned about reports that certain fanatical Nazis intended to retreat to a 'National Redoubt' in the Austrian Alps and fight to the death. Intelligence suggested that tons of arms and ammunition had been taken to the redoubt, and that they would be used to launch attacks on Allied occupation forces in the weeks, months and even years after the war ended. These so-called 'werewolves' were to be led by Ernst Kaltenbrunner, the man who took over direct control of the Gestapo after the assassination of Reinhard Heydrich in 1942.

The hunt for Kaltenbrunner was intensified when his Gestapo chief in Vienna, SS Brigadier General Huber, was found in early May in a hospital in the Altaussee district of Austria. Huber admitted he had been sheltered by Kaltenbrunner, and soon local Resistance informants passed on the news that Kaltenbrunner had been spotted in a remote mountain cabin called Wildensee Huette. An American soldier dressed in traditional Austrian lederhosen and hat approached the cabin posing as a mountain hiker. When he discovered there were indeed

Germans hiding inside it, the cabin was surrounded by armed troops. Kaltenbrunner and three other SS men initially elected to fight but upon realizing the hopelessness of their situation decided to surrender. The Gestapo chief was carrying false papers and posing as a doctor, complete with full medical kit.

After interrogation by the Americans confirmed his true identity, Kaltenbrunner was flown to a British interrogation centre where he received harsh and unsympathetic treatment. As a consequence, he refused to co-operate with his questioners and denied all connections with the Nazi regime. His uncompromising attitude resulted in him being taken for trial at Nuremberg in handcuffs – the only one of the 21 major defendants to be treated in this manner.

Perhaps the greatest mystery left unsolved after the end of the war is the fate of 'Gestapo Müller', head of the organization and intimately involved in the very worst of their crimes. He is said to have been at Hitler's side in the Führerbunker just two days before the Nazi leader committed suicide. He remains officially missing, though a detailed report by the Americans concluded that he was probably killed in Berlin either shortly before the end of the war or very soon after it ended. However, a grave in Berlin said to contain his body was opened 30 years after the end of the war and found to contain two unknown soldiers rather than Müller.

The US records contain cryptic and conflicting hints of other possible fates. One former Nazi interviewed in December 1945 stated that Müller escaped Berlin via a secret underground passage. Reports from the Russian zone of Berlin suggested that he shot himself and his entire family two days before Hitler died. Remarkably, according to the US's own records, it appears that Müller was in their custody in a camp in Altenstadt in Upper Bavaria in December 1945. No details of what happened to him after this were recorded, though the card bore the words: 'Case closed 29th January 1946'. This has led some to speculate that Müller was secretly flown to the United States and employed by the American intelligence services.

This is less improbable than it first appears: the US Office of Strategic Services (OSS) was keen to prevent senior German scientific and military figures from being captured by the Soviets after the end of the war in Europe. Once key scientists such as Wernher von Braun had been debriefed, it became clear that their knowledge might help shorten the war in the Pacific, not least by potentially helping with the atomic bomb project. Stalin's Soviet military machine was already seen as a threat to the Allies, so senior German military leaders were highly prized for the intelligence they had on Soviet operations.

Ernst Kaltenbrunner

Ernst Kaltenbrunner took over as Chief of the Reich Security Main Office (*Reichssicherheitshauptamt*, or RSHA) after the assassination of Reinhard Heydrich in 1942. Born in Austria in 1903, he was physically imposing at 1.9 m (6 ft 4 in), and it is said that even Himmler feared him. His reputation for rounding up and executing suspects without trial reached its zenith after the failed plot to assassinate Hitler in 1944. He hatched his own plots to assassinate Churchill, Roosevelt and Stalin, and headed up an underground force of 'stay-behind' agents who were tasked with sabotaging Allied occupation forces in the event of Germany losing the war. He was executed in 1946 after being found guilty of war crimes.

The US officially launched 'Operation Paperclip' to round up a list of key German personnel in March 1946. This, however, was an extension of an operation that had begun even before the war had ended. Nuclear physicist Werner Heisenberg was arrested two days before Germany surrendered, in territory still controlled by German forces. He and countless others were captured during 'Operation Alsos', which directly targeted the Reich's nuclear scientists. The rocket scientists at the Baltic-coast German Army Research Centre at Peenemünde were taken into custody in July 1945 as a result of 'Operation Overcast'. Many more top figures willingly handed themselves over to the Allies rather than chance their luck with the Red Army. Others still used 'rat lines' to escape from Germany, often with the collaboration of Allied secret services.

The infamous Gestapo chief Klaus Barbie was one such escapee. The 'Butcher of Lyon' was employed by the US Counter Intelligence Corps despite having been tried *in absentia* in France and found guilty of crimes against humanity. At his trial, countless witnesses described how he had tortured them with his own hands, and he was implicated in the deaths of some 4,000 members of the French Resistance. Nonetheless, the United States aided him in escaping to Bolivia, where he was provided with a new identity and allegedly assisted in the capture and execution of Che Guevara.

It is a grim irony of the war that the Allied 'T-Forces' sent to capture German scientists adopted tactics unnervingly similar to those deployed by the Gestapo. They usually arrived in the dead of night and with no prior warning. Providing no evidence of their identity, the T-Force men would bundle their captives away and provide no information to relatives on where the men were being taken, or why. Around 1,500 Germans are estimated to have been abducted in such circumstances by the British alone.

Even some of the most infamous Gestapo war criminals were protected if they proved useful in the new 'Cold War' with the Soviet Union. Major Horst Kopkow was seized by British military policemen on 29 May 1945 in a village on the Baltic coast. Kopkow had been responsible for the Gestapo's counter-espionage and counter-sabotage operations and was implicated in the deaths of hundreds of SOE agents, including such famous names as Violette Szabo and Noor Inayat Khan. But he was also the 'desk murderer' who helped destroy the Soviet Red Orchestra espionage ring, and had crucial information relating to Soviet spies and double agents in the West. The British faked his death for him in 1948 and protected him from the war crimes tribunal in return for his intelligence. He was later given a new identity as a textile factory worker in the British zone of West Germany, and remained under the protection of British intelligence until his death in 1996.

Not all of those who escaped Germany after the war lived happily ever after, however. Adolf Eichmann, the man whom Heydrich entrusted to put into practice the 'Final Solution', adopted the name of 'Otto Eckmann' in 1945. He was arrested by the Americans and held in a camp for SS officers, but his captors had no idea of their prisoner's true identity. Before they could establish who he was, Eichmann escaped and fled to Austria. He lived there undetected for five years, posing as a forestry worker and later leasing a small parcel of land.

While the jury at Nuremberg was hearing testimony of the atrocities he had organized, Eichmann was busy conspiring to escape once more, this time to Argentina. With the help of Austrian cleric Bishop Alois Hudal, he obtained false papers under the name of 'Ricardo Klement'. Hudal was a known Nazi sympathizer who organized one of the key 'rat-lines' used by senior figures of the Third Reich to escape justice. In addition to Eichmann, he also assisted Josef Mengele (the 'Angel of Death' at Auschwitz), Captain Eduard Roschmann (the 'Butcher of Riga') and countless others.

Eichmann took a ship from Genoa to Argentina in

1950 and became department head at Mercedes-Benz in Buenos Aires. Confident of his safety, he began to give interviews to sympathetic journalists and his son Klaus boasted publicly of his father's exploits during the war. Via the dogged Nazi-hunter Simon Wiesenthal, news of Eichmann's whereabouts reached the Israeli secret service, Mossad. On 11 May 1960 they kidnapped him, returned with him to Israel and put him on trial. On 15 December 1961 he was found guilty of war crimes and crimes against humanity, and sentenced to death. He was hanged on 1 June 1962.

Martin Bormann, Joseph Goebbels and countless others elected to follow Hitler's lead and commit suicide rather than stand trial for their crimes. But many of the key Gestapo figures were arrested in due course and would stand trial in public at Nuremberg. Rudolph Diels, one-time head of the Gestapo, surrendered to American troops on 10 April 1945. He had been arrested by his former colleagues in the wake of the 1944 assassination plot against Hitler and held in 'protective custody' for several months. In March 1945 he was released to an SS Punishment Battalion and sent to the Western Front near Mainz. He became ill with tuberculosis and was moved to a hospital in Hanover, where he remained until the war came to an end. Diels would become a chief witness for the prosecution in Nuremberg.

Adolf Eichmann

Eichmann was the 'Jewish Specialist' employed by Reinhard Heydrich to investigate solutions to the Nazis' 'Jewish Problem'. Born in 1906, he was one of the chief architects of the 'Final Solution', which involved the extermination of Jews in concentration camps. Originally, he conceived of sending the Jewish population abroad to Poland or Madagascar, but the plan was never implemented. When Nazi leaders witnessed first-hand the initial mass executions of Jews by firing squads, they determined to find a more 'humane' method of murder, and settled upon the idea of gas chambers. Eichmann proved himself to be horribly efficient at organizing the transportation of hundreds of thousands of Jews to such chambers at Sobibor, Chelmno, Treblinka and Auschwitz. His enthusiasm for the task became legendary – even after Himmler had ordered him to cease deportations, Eichmann sent a further 50,000 Hungarian Jews on an eight-day death march to Austria.

After the war, Eichmann fled to Argentina and lived under the assumed name of Ricardo Klement until he was captured by Mossad agents in 1960. He was kidnapped and taken to Israel, where he was tried and sentenced to death for crimes against humanity. He was hanged at Ramleh Prison in 1962.

Rudolf Diels

A protégé of Hermann Göring, Rudolf Diels was head of the Gestapo during 1933 and 1934, having been head of the Prussian Political Police when Hitler came to power. He was the main interrogator in the investigation into the Reichstag Fire in 1933. Though considered competent, he was never ruthless or fanatical enough to hang on to power and fell victim to the political machinations of Himmler, who took control of the Gestapo in 1934. Diels survived the war and worked in local government until his retirement in 1953. He died in a hunting accident four years later.

The Nuremberg Trials

It was not just senior individuals such as Göring and Kaltenbrunner who went on trial in Nuremberg in 1945 and 1946: the entire Gestapo organization was alleged to be criminal, along with the SD, SA and SS. Described as 'the greatest trial in history' by Norman Birkett, one of the British judges who presided over it, the military tribunals that began on 20 November 1945 saw 23 of the most senior figures of the Third Reich called to account for their actions. Martin Bormann was tried *in absentia* and Robert Ley committed suicide just a week into proceedings, while Kaltenbrunner was absent for long periods due to illness.

Göring blamed Himmler for most of the Gestapo's atrocities and repeatedly attempted to distance himself from the organization he himself had founded. He bombastically presented himself as a patriotic German and was defiant, even brilliant, when defending his own record and the aims and objectives of the Third Reich. But his defence was undone by his own frank admissions of criminal behaviour and he became more subdued when confronted with images from the concentration camps, and the hundreds of pages of testimony on mass executions carried out by the Nazis. He was also badly shaken by the evidence of prosecutor David Maxwell-Fyfe, who proved beyond doubt that Göring knew about the executions of the Stalag

Senior Nazis on trial in 1946. The Gestapo's creator Hermann Göring is seated at the left of the front row. Beside him are Rudolph Hess, Joachim von Ribbentrop, Wilheim Keitel and chief of the RSHA Ernst Kaltenbrunner.

Luft III escapers and did nothing to prevent them. The trial lasted 218 days and, given the overwhelming evidence against him, the verdict was inevitable:

There is nothing to be said in mitigation. For Göring was often, indeed almost always, the moving force, second only to his leader. He was the leading war aggressor, both as political and as military leader; he was the director of the slave labour programme and the creator of the oppressive programme against the Jews and other races, at home and abroad.... His guilt is unique in its enormity. The record discloses no excuses for this man.

He was sentenced to hang, and the court refused his request to be shot instead. In the event, Göring did indeed get to choose the manner of his death: he swallowed potassium cyanide the night before he was due to be executed. How he obtained the poison remains a mystery, but the most likely explanation is that he bribed one of his American guards.

The evidence against Kaltenbrunner was more directly associated with the evidence against the Gestapo itself. Colonel Robert G. Storey put forward compelling evidence of the horrific crimes committed by the organization under the stewardship of first Heydrich and later Kaltenbrunner. He outlined the scale of the operation, indicating that 40,000 to 50,000 people were employed as Gestapo agents by the end of the war. Given that the Gestapo worked hand in glove with the Kripo and SD for many of its functions, and that each office had hundreds of informants on its books, it is clear that it cast a net very widely over the Reich.

The infamous *Einsatz* groups or *Einsatzkommandos* were clearly demonstrated to have been controlled by the Gestapo, and details of the hundreds of thousands of civilian murders for which they were responsible were heard. Even the Nazi commissioner of the territory of Sluzk, it was revealed, objected to the behaviour of the *Einsatz* groups in his territory, and wrote a scathing report on the matter to the Commissioner General of Minsk. The report was read aloud to the tribunal, to provide a snapshot of just one operation carried out in 1941:

... As regards the execution of the action, I must point out, to my deepest regret, that the latter almost bordered on sadism. The town itself during the action offered a picture of horror. With indescribable brutality on the part both of the German police officers and particularly of the Lithuanian partisans, the Jewish people, and also with them White Ruthenians, were taken out of their dwellings and herded together. Everywhere in the town shots were to be heard, and in different streets the corpses of Jews who had been shot accumulated.... To have buried alive seriously wounded people, who then worked their way out of their graves again, is such extreme beastliness that this incident as such must be reported to the Führer.

The details of how prisoners at Mauthausen camp were executed were also revealed: those condemned were 'measured' in a specially designed machine, which fired a bullet into the victim's neck as soon as the moving plank determining his height touched the top of his head. If a lack of time prevented this method being used, then prisoners were taken to a shower room that allowed either water or gas to be passed through its pipes. Colonel Storey's closing remarks to the tribunal can hardly be improved upon as a summary of the organization's brutality:

Its methods were utterly ruthless. It operated outside the law and sent its victims to the concentration camps. The term 'Gestapo' became the symbol of the Nazi regime of force and terror. Behind the scenes operating secretly, the SD, through its vast network of informants, spied upon the German people in their daily lives, on the streets, in the shops, and even within the sanctity of the churches. The most casual remark of the German citizen might bring him before the Gestapo where his fate and freedom were decided without recourse to law. In this government, in which the rule of law was replaced by a tyrannical rule of men, the Gestapo was the primary instrumental of oppression.

The Gestapo and the SD played an important part in almost every criminal act of the conspiracy. The category of these crimes, apart from the thousands of specific instances of torture and cruelty in policing Germany for the benefit of the conspirators, reads like a page from the devil's notebook:

They fabricated the border incidents which Hitler used as an excuse for attacking Poland.

They murdered hundreds of thousands of defenceless men, women, and children by the infamous Einsatz groups.

They removed Jews, political leaders, and scientists from prisoner-of-war camps and murdered them.

They took recaptured prisoners of war to concentration camps and murdered them.

They established and classified the concentration camps and sent thousands of people into them for extermination and slave labour.

They cleared Europe of the Jews and were responsible for sending hundreds of thousands to their deaths in annihilation camps.

They rounded up hundreds of thousands of citizens of occupied countries and shipped them to Germany for forced labour and sent slave labourers to labour reformatory camps.

They executed captured commandos and paratroopers and protected civilians who lynched allied fliers.

They took civilians of occupied countries to Germany for secret trial and punishment.

They arrested, tried, and punished citizens of occupied countries under special criminal procedures, which did not accord fair trials, and by summary methods.

They murdered or sent to concentration camps the relatives of persons who had allegedly committed crimes.

They ordered the murder of prisoners in Sipo and SD prisons to prevent their release by Allied armies.

They participated in the seizure and spoliation of public and private property.

They were primary agencies for the persecution of the Jews and churches.

Kaltenbrunner was found guilty and executed, along with nine other senior Nazis, on 16 October 1946. The entire Gestapo organization was also found to be criminal in nature. At the Nuremberg trials, thousands of victims of the Gestapo had their stories told to the world, and received a measure of justice. Hundreds of thousands more, however, lie in unmarked graves having suffered untold horrors at the hands of Hitler's secret terror police.

As the French Resistance hero Georges Bidault said after the war was over:

Freedom is when one hears the bell at seven o'clock in the morning and knows it is the milkman and not the Gestapo.

Index